Individualizing
Instruction
and Keeping
Your Sanity

Individualizing Instruction and Keeping Your Sanity

William M. Bechtol, Ed.D.

*Director of the Center for
the Management of Educational Systems
Southwest Minnesota State College*

Follett Publishing Company/Chicago

CONTENTS

Introduction

"The teacher seems to forget that I'm just me. We're so busy. First it's reading groups, then our phonics workbook, then English, then spelling . . . I raise my hand and she says, 'Not now, Jimmy. It's almost time for mathematics'!"

"Jimmy used to like school. This year . . . well, I don't know. He's smart enough, but the program just doesn't seem to fit him."

"There are twenty-eight students in my room. Of course I know that each one is a unique, different individual. I just don't have time to individualize twenty-eight programs."

"Our community would chase me out if we tried to individualize instruction. It's tough enough to be principal of the school the way it is."

These statements sound familiar, don't they? What they all reflect is the need for individualized instruction. Students, parents, teachers, and principals want to individualize instruction, but most of them simply don't know how; they don't have the necessary skills.

The purpose of this book is to help teachers and administrators develop the skills needed to individualize instruction. It is a source book for changing a school from a traditional program to a system that individualizes and humanizes education. It provides a plan for "putting children first."

In designing an individualized instruction program, three questions must be answered:

What student outcomes are desired?

What kind of school provides the conditions to bring about these outcomes?

What competencies are needed by teachers to bring about these outcomes?

This book focuses on all three questions. It presents a total program for individualizing instruction.

The desired student outcomes must be determined by a teacher, a teaching team, a faculty, a community, or a combination of some or all of these. This book provides a system for identifying what a student should know and be able to do.

Three models of the kind of school that provides the conditions for individualizing instruction are described in this book: (1) the continuous progress, or nongraded, model; (2) the open school model, of which the British Infant School is an example; and (3) the Individually Guided Education (IGE) model. Each of these models is so structured that it provides an appropriate organization for individualizing instruction.

Many of the competencies needed by teachers to individualize instruction have been identified. This book defines some of these competencies and describes ways teachers in individualized schools use them. Among these competencies are criterion-referenced teaching, assessment strategies, identification of students' learning styles, the use of different learning modes, the selection of diversified learning activities, management strategies, and systems for reporting student progress. An in-service training program to develop these competencies is included in Chapter 10. In addition, the competency packages (compacs) developed for the competency-based teacher education program at Southwest Minnesota State College are included as appendixes. These appendixes detail a program for gaining additional skills with which to individualize instruction.

The need for individualization cannot be overemphasized. Schools must provide for the individual differences of students. It is my hope that this book will help teachers, administrators, and laymen build individualized instruction programs—and keep their sanity while doing so.

One gives up many interesting things while writing a book. This task would never have been completed without the help and encouragement of many people. I would like to acknowledge and thank Frank Nauyokas, IGE League Facilitator in southwest Minnesota, and Lowell Tornquist, Director of the Center for Applied Instruction at Southwest Minnesota State College, for their suggestions on the manuscript; Norman Graper, Principal of Wilson School in Janesville, Wisconsin, for his challenging ideas; the IGE teachers and administrators in southwest Minnesota for sharing their ideas with me and trying out some of mine; the education students at Southwest Minnesota State College for field testing many of the ideas; students, parents, teachers, and administrators for ideas, support, and encouragement; Jack Hutchinson and Sharon Olsen of Follett Publishing Company for believing that these individualizing concepts should be shared; and Dianne Vonderharr for her excellent typing and proofing.

Most thanks must be expressed to my family, who also gave up many interesting things so that Dad could spend evenings and weekends writing in the study. This book is dedicated to my wife, Mildred, and my children, Bill, Jr., Susan, and Bob.

William M. Bechtol
Marshall, Minnesota
June, 1973

Children, like fingerprints, are all different.

Chapter 1
Why Individualize, Anyway?

For more years than one cares to remember, we educators have been giving lip service to the concept of taking a youngster where he is and helping him to develop to his optimum. For the same span of time we have been kidding ourselves. In actual practice, very little has been done in taking a student where he is. Too often we herd youngsters into the same classroom because they are all ten years old, for instance, and have been in school for four years. Then we expect each student to master the work assigned to him in this classroom. All the time that we are doing this, we are reminding ourselves of the importance of recognizing individual differences in children. These are the kinds of inconsistencies that are evident in our schools today.

Despite the Winnetka Plan, the Dalton Plan, Project PLAN, non-graded schools (sometimes called ungrading), differentiated staffing, and all the other attempts by school staffs to cope with individual differences among children, the sad truth is that teaching in the United States is now and has been essentially for groups, not individuals. We hear statements or questions such as: "I can keep all four of my social studies sections on the same page." "All the kids in our city started the third primer today." "But, Mrs. Miller, if you teach some of your fifth-grade students from the sixth-grade mathematics book, what will I do with them next year?"

Most of us who have been teaching in the past few years have tried to individualize our instructional programs. I shall never forget my first experience. In my self-contained classroom, I tried to permit students to move at their own speed through a mathematics textbook and workbook. I have never been so frustrated in my life. Most of the time I felt I was the only one in the room working. All the kids were standing in line waiting for me to help them or to tell them what to do next.

You have undoubtedly had similar experiences. Yet instructional programs can be individualized. And my travels to schools throughout the United States have convinced me that people want individualized instruction.

Children want individualized instruction.

Parents want individualized instruction.

Teachers want to individualize instruction.

Principals want to individualize instruction.

Why, then, is the traditional graded, self-contained classroom the most common instructional plan found in elementary schools today? Why do we not individualize instruction today? Most of us do not know how! We do not have the skills to individualize instruction.

The purpose of this book is to help teachers and administrators develop these needed skills. It is a source book for changing a school with a traditional program to a school with a program that individualizes and humanizes education.

Each Child Is Different

Why do we want to individualize? Why is there a movement across the United States to individualize instruction? The answer is simple, but the solution is difficult. *Children, like fingerprints, are all different.* They just do not fit the lockstep structure that is currently used in most elementary schools today.

Children really are different. We know that if a teacher deals with 300 students each year for forty years—and that is a long teaching career—she will never encounter any two children who are precisely alike. If this teacher were able to teach 12 million or 12 billion human beings instead of 12 thousand, the same would be true. The uniqueness of the individual is a fundamental principle of life.[1]

Children differ anatomically, physiologically, and biochemically from one another. Organs of the body differ markedly in size and shape. The chemical composition of body fluids shows considerable variation. Heart rate, respiration rate, and other such processes show the same variabilities. In short, if we consider these characteristics, there is no "normal" person who might serve as a medical standard or model.[2]

In an individualized teaching program, it is recognized that there is no standard student. Each student is a unique individual who learns in his own way and in his own time. In changing from a traditional program to an individualized program, one school system examined student achievement. The differences in achievement of students of the same age and the differences in individual students' scores on achievement subtests were used as the rationale for individualizing instruction.

Two reasons that schools are moving toward individualized instruction stand out.

The first is that every class is really nongraded. Look at the reading scores in Figure 1. The norm of this group should be, according to graded standards, sixth grade, first month. In the suburban community studied, the norm was seventh grade, sixth month; only 25 of the 160 students tested, or 15.6 percent, actually scored within the sixth grade. The rest scored either higher or lower.

Fig. 1. Reading Achievement Range of Sixth Graders in Tipp City, Ohio

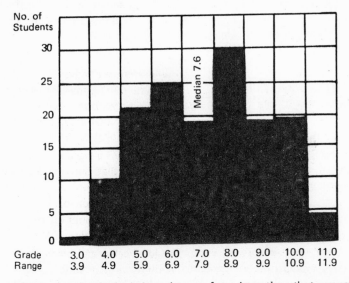

Teachers and principals have known for a long time that a range exists in any class, but they act as if this were not true. Many teachers treat all students as if they were the same. They say, "You're not acting like a fifth grader," or, "That's not sixth-grade work" (whatever that means).[3]

Traditional teachers look upon the class, grade, or group as an entity. Each student is presumed to have relatively equal learning needs, abilities, and responses. The traditional school is teacher-paced and scheduled to meet the convenience of the school and community. Students in the same classroom who are taught by traditional methods are generally given the same assignment, regardless of their individual capabilities or progress.[4]

Students who test much higher or lower than the norm are often treated incorrectly. An elementary school student whose test scores show that he is capable of reading high school materials is rewarded with an A for work that is probably too easy for him. He hears his teachers say such things as, "Good work! You made the honor roll." In reality, the youngster may not have been working much at all.

How about the other students? How do we treat the student whose performance is average or well below the grade that he is in?

A track coach would not require every child to run a five-minute mile simply because the child was eleven years old, for example. He would know that while some eleven-year-olds could perform the task, and a few might even surpass it, still others would be unable to achieve it. He would know that the skills and stamina involved are not factors of chronological age alone. In the same way, to insist that every student complete and master a sixth-grade reader by June of his sixth year in school is unrealistic and unfair.

With the student who is functioning well below the grade norm, we often do even more wrong. To expect more than is reasonable is bad enough, but to see parents and teachers react to a student's failure as if the student and not the system is wrong is even worse. How many times have we asked a failing student to try harder? One reason that schools choose to move to individualized programs is that students the same age and in the same class function in many, many grades.

The second reason for moving toward individualized instruction is that an individual student tests in different grades for different subjects. In Figure 2, individual test scores for three sixth graders (from the group in Figure 1) are compared; in Figure 3, test scores for three sophomores are compared. All tested in at least three different grades. For a sixth-grade student to test seventh grade in spelling, fifth grade in reading, and fourth grade in arithmetic is not unusual. The problem is that none of his sixth-grade materials happens to fit him. The second reason, then, is that a child within himself is non-graded.[5]

Fig. 2. Grade Levels of Three Tipp City (Ohio) Sixth Graders by Subject

Subject	Pupil		
	A	B	C
Reading vocabulary	5.7	7.7	10.0
Reading comprehension	3.6	7.2	10.1
Arithmetic reasoning	6.3	7.5	6.8
Arithmetic fundamentals	5.3	5.4	7.2
English	4.8	6.8	6.2
Spelling	4.8	6.5	7.0

Fig. 3. Grade Levels of Three Tipp City (Ohio) High School Sophomores by Subject

Subject	Pupil		
	A	B	C
Reading vocabulary	15.4	9.6	12.1
Reading comprehension	15.4	9.5	12.1
Arithmetic reasoning	15.7	11.0	10.6
Arithmetic fundamentals	16.0	12.2	9.2
English	15.3	12.4	12.2
Spelling	16.0	8.0	14.3

These two differences in student achievement are only indications of the individual differences of children. Psychological individuality is of the greatest importance to education. No matter how carefully students are selected for a homogeneous group, each student will react in his own unique way. There are differences in talents and aptitudes, in interests and motives, and in habits and response styles.[6]

Tunnel Vision

One of the problems in individualizing instruction is our tunnel vision, our preconceived idea of how an elementary school should look. With our tunnel vision we see a teacher in front of a class of thirty students. We see the teacher lecturing. We see all the students using the same book and working on the same page. The individualized instruction program is well outside the parameters of this tunnel vision.

In the team-taught, nongraded, multi-age-group school where I worked as an elementary principal, we had many visitors. Each Thursday, visiting teams came from all over the United States to see our program in action. Before each visiting team entered our classrooms, we had a briefing session and tried to explain what the visitors would see. Then they observed students working in small groups, working in pairs, and interacting independently with learning packages or at learning stations. Teachers moved easily through open space classrooms, helping individual students, checking student progress, leading small groups. Rarely did the visitors see and hear a teacher "lecturing." In the afternoon, the visitors returned to the office for a debriefing session. Often one of the visitors would comment, "You know what I'd like to do? I'd like to come back some day when your teachers are teaching."

That is what is meant by tunnel vision. We must help students, parents, teachers, and principals understand how a program of individualized instruction looks and works.

Goals of Individualization

Schools exist for children. All that is done to establish and maintain schools must be measured in terms of what is best for each child. Systems that attempt to individualize instruction do so to provide appropriate learning experiences for each learner in the school.

There are four major goals that schools organized for individualized programs attempt to achieve.

The first goal is to translate traditional skills and subject matter into behavioral objectives so that the diagnostic-prescriptive approach can be used. In other words, the "stuff" that has traditionally been taught in the elementary school is translated into behavioral terms. The traditional elementary subjects, such as reading, writing, and arithmetic, are taught in an instructional program that uses pre-assessment, diversified learning materials, different learning modes, and post-assessment. Mastery learning is emphasized. The concept of mastery may be the key to the movement toward individualized instruction.*

The second goal is to use individualization to improve the self-concept of each student, to make a student feel good about himself while he is in the learning process. This is most frequently done by establishing close student-teacher relationships that focus on the learner's needs. The importance of human relationships is emphasized. A good teaching team can match appropriate learning activities with a student's interests and needs, permitting the student to experience daily success. It is amazing how turned on a student can get when he works in a program that he understands.

The third goal is to help each student develop the skills to be a lifelong independent learner. The knowledge explosion has made it impossible to "cover" a subject. I have seen a teacher who "covered" all the countries in Europe in a two-week unit. I saw another teacher assign the War of 1812 on Tuesday and the Panic of 1819 and the election of 1824 on Wednesday. The focus in an individualized program is on teaching learning skills, which many schools fail to do. Knowing how to learn is more important than a thousand memorized facts. Study skills, independent learning, and inquiry learning become much more valuable if the student is to continue learning after he leaves school. (I am reminded of the teacher who got her master's degree in literature and swore she would never read a book again.) The individualized program is designed so that students have the skills and the desire to learn after they leave school, as well as while they are there.

The fourth goal is to provide a relevant curriculum. Students throughout the country have been demanding different curricula. In an individualized program that emphasizes the processes of learning, the choice of subject matter is not nearly so important as the skills taught. A student may, for example, choose to classify simple machines, animals, library books, or bubble gum cards, depending upon his interests, but he must learn to classify. Student interest is the key in selecting content. Therefore, in addition to being a diagnostician and prescriber, the teacher becomes a facilitator. The teacher assumes a role similar to that of a travel agent. The student

---

*The criteria for mastery as the term is used in this book are (1) what is mastered is retained; (2) what is mastered is used as a stepping stone to higher work; (3) a student can use what is mastered in situations where the knowledge is appropriate; and (4) a student gains a sense of gratification from knowing that he has mastered something.

says, "Here's what I'd like to study." The teacher says, "Here are some ways you can do it."

These are the goals of an individualized school program, a program in which the individual differences of students are accepted. Such a program provides a structure that permits each youngster to develop to his optimum.

Individually Guided Education accepts nongraded schools, team teaching, multi-age grouping, differentiated staffing, and diagnostic-prescriptive teaching, not as innovations, but as the way schools ought to be organized.

Chapter 2
What an Individualized System Is

While directing a study to develop a nongraded program from kindergarten through senior high school, I had a chance to visit more than forty of the "best" schools in the United States. The visiting team I worked with spent a lot of time studying innovative school programs. Two stories are appropriate here because they relate to what we found.

Story One is about Zeke. One warm afternoon, Zeke was cutting wood in a Kentucky hollow. The only sound he heard was his own ax cutting the wood. Then he heard a rumble. It sounded as if it were far off—way up the hill. The rumble came closer and closer. Zeke was scared. He didn't know what the sound was, and he was in the hollow all by himself. So he hid behind the woodpile and peered out to see what was making the noise. He saw his friend Luke pulling a big contraption down the hill. Luke was in an awkward position. He was pulling the contraption and at the same time turning a big crank. Zeke came out from behind the woodpile and ran up to Luke.

"What is that thing?" he asked.

Luke replied, "It's a rock crusher."

"Oh, do you have any rocks in it?"

"No," replied Luke, "it's so hard to pull and turn at the same time that I haven't had time to put rocks in it."

That's Story One.

Story Two[1] is about something many readers are too young to remember: World War II. During that time before television, people listened to radio, and they worried about rationing. Lots of things were rationed—meat, sugar, tires, and gasoline, among other things.

One of the key rationing problems was butter. Many families just did not have enough butter to last them through the week. The radio show called "Answerman" tried to handle this problem.

Mrs. Housewife said, "My problem is that we run out of butter each week. What can I do to make our butter ration last longer?"

Mr. Answerman said, "You simply take a pound of butter and mix it with a pound of lard."

"Oh," said Mrs. Housewife, "how does it look?"

"Just like butter."

"How does it spread?"

"Just like butter."

"How does it taste?"

"Just like lard."

That's Story Two!

When you visit forty schools, you find many that claim to be individualized, but some of them are like the empty rock crusher. There are no rocks in the crusher; nothing new is happening to boys and girls. Other schools that claim to be individualized "taste" just like traditional schools. They claim their programs are butter, but they taste like lard.

The system for individualizing instruction described in this book is different. It does have something in it, and new things do happen to children.

There are three models for individualized instruction that are appropriate for elementary schools. They are (1) the continuous progress, or nongraded, model; (2) the open school, or British Infant School, model; and (3) the Individually Guided Education (IGE) model.

The Continuous Progress Model

The continuous progress, or nongraded, model began to emerge when educators started questioning the graded system. An alarming number of students were failed (not promoted) each year. At the same time, educators were apprehensive because bright students were being restricted to unchallenging situations. Plans to alter the organization of the graded school began to appear in the early 1900s. The Winnetka Plan and the Dalton Plan are the best known of these developments. The modern conception of the nongraded school began in 1934.[2] Milwaukee adopted a nongraded program in 1942.[3] In 1964, the National Education Association's Education

Research Service, in a postcard survey, discovered that nearly one-third of the school systems reporting had one or more nongraded schools.[4]

The work of Drs. John I. Goodlad and Robert Anderson and the publication of their classic book, *The Nongraded Elementary School,* in 1959 did more to disseminate the nongraded concept than any other single act. Nongraded schools emerged all over the United States. Schools in Garden Springs, Kentucky; Melbourne, Florida; Newton, Rhode Island; Plainview-Old Bethpage, New York; and Tipp City, Ohio, were among those that received national publicity for nongraded programs.[5]

Nongrading is a vertical pattern of school organization. In the traditional graded school, students of the same age move together at a regular pace from kindergarten through grade 12, one grade a year. In a nongraded school, students progress at their own individual rates according to their abilities.

In a nongraded "birthday school," for example, the school superintendent would send a child a card on the child's fifth birthday. The card would read: "Happy Birthday! We'll see you in school tomorrow." And the next day the child would enter kindergarten. This change would permit students to enter kindergarten all the time. Then, when the kindergarten teacher thought that the child was ready to begin reading, he would leave kindergarten. In a short time students of many different ages would be at many different levels—each at the one that was right for him. The yearly progression system of the graded program would be broken.

The implications of nongraded elementary schools may only be known when students from them enter high school. There it becomes evident that in mathematics, for instance, the students' knowledge varies from decimal fractions to Algebra II, depending on each student's individual learning rate.

While visiting a Florida school that has a continuous progress program from nursery school through junior college, we were guided through the campus by the captain of the high school football team. We asked, "Larry, what grade are you in?"

He laughed and said, "Well, I haven't taken senior government because if I complete that course I'll graduate. And if I graduate, I won't be eligible for spring sports, and my coach says that later I might have a chance for a baseball scholarship."

We visited with him more and discovered that almost all his work was at the junior college level. He was in a school that gave a student the right to be a part-time high school senior and a part-time college freshman.

The continuous progress model is more than a plan for vertical movement, however. Frank Dufay, principal of the Ungraded School, Plainview, Long Island, has identified the following characteristics of a nongraded school: (1) it has continuous student progress; (2) it provides flexibility in grouping by removing grade labels; (3) it is designed to facilitate the teacher's role in providing for students' individual differences; and (4) it eliminates or lessens the problem of retention or acceleration.[6]

The continuous progress model today is demonstrated through curriculum programs such as Individually Prescribed Instruction (IPI) or Project PLAN and through continuous progress levels that have been developed by local school staffs.

The Open School Model

The open school model has received much publicity recently. Open classroom teaching begins with the assumption that children want to learn and will learn in their own fashion. The components of the British Infant School, an open school, include (1) "family" grouping, or pairing or multi-age grouping within a classroom; (2) an integrated day; (3) team teaching; (4) an open learning environment; and (5) individualized instruction.

Open education is not permissive education. There *is* structure involved. Open education is an attitude. Students are trusted and given responsibility.[7] The teacher assesses what a student already knows and works with him to help him select what he will learn next. And both student and parents have a voice in what happens.

The environment of an open school is rich and diverse. Every nook and cranny is used. If the building is old, you may find coat closets have been adapted to provide retreats and playhouses. Walls have been knocked out. In a new school building, it is difficult to tell where one classroom begins and another ends. Space is divided functionally, and students move in and out of it according to the work they are doing. The open school is a masterpiece of the teachers' ingenuity. Common objects are seized upon as raw materials for play, work, and learning. From dog biscuits to buttons, objects are used for classification, counting, and art work, for example. There are dress-up corners, kitchens, carpentry areas, science areas—all designed for students' work and play, which in

England are regarded as seriously as traditional classroom subjects are.[8] Reading, writing, numbers, and art are of prime importance in the open classroom. Students read. They write. They do art work.

In England, teachers determine and control the curriculum. Governing bodies, such as boards of education, seldom interfere. The head teacher teaches. She is not viewed by other teachers as a member of the enemy camp, as many teachers view the American elementary school principal. Parents in England would not consider complaining to a board or the central office. Teachers, not boards or textbook companies, make decisions about instructional programs. American education would require a great deal of restructuring to be organized like the British Infant School.[9]

Many American schools experience difficulty in implementing the British Infant School model. There are three reasons for this. First, American teachers have not been given, or they have not accepted, responsibility for determining instructional programs. Second, American principals view themselves as administrators, managers, or educational leaders; they do not see themselves as head teachers. Third, many of the procedures followed in American elementary schools seem to be based on a lack of trust. For example, not even restroom breaks (obviously an individual activity) have been individualized; students are lined up for restroom breaks. And because they are not trusted, the students become very creative at the "restroom game."

The individualized model proposed in this book emphasizes many of the components of the open school. It is my hope that the open school concept will help American teachers and principals learn to trust students, to develop an open learning environment, and to assume greater roles in determining instructional programs.

Individually Guided Education

Individually Guided Education (IGE) is a comprehensive program for formulating and carrying out instruction for individual students. It is a system for improving instruction. It provides for variations in what each student should learn, how rapidly he should learn it, and how he should go about learning. Designers of IGE programs believe that for higher learner achievement to be realized, each student's characteristics must be taken into account.[10]

Individually Guided Education combines behavioral learning objectives, assessment, a multimedia environment, and each student's learning style to permit elementary school staffs to make education appropriate for the individual learners in their schools.[11]

It is my opinion that the IGE model (*see* Figure 4) contains components of both the continuous progress model and the open school model, that it provides an appropriate marriage of both models, and that it is easier to implement than either of the other two. Therefore, this book emphasizes the skills and processes needed in IGE schools. These skills and processes, however, are appropriate for any program of individualized instruction. They can be used in an open school, in a continuous progress school, or in a program designed by a local school staff.

Fig. 4. The IGE Learning Cycle

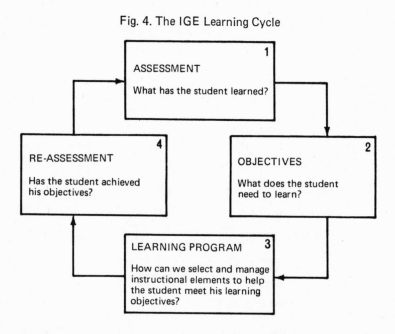

The Research Behind IGE

The key research that has effected the organization of the individualized elementary school was done by the Wisconsin Research and Development Center for Cognitive Learning at the University of Wisconsin. Dr. Herbert J. Klausmier led the team that developed the Multi-unit/IGE School. This team first looked at what was going on in elementary schools today. At first they thought that most teachers and principals were spending their time maintaining instructional programs as good as those in the past.[12] Then they discovered that school staffs were concerned because falling reading and mathematics achievement test scores gave some indication that they were *not* maintaining as good a program.

The research and development staff began to ask what the function of the elementary school in the decades ahead should be. Five functions were identified for the schools of the 1970s and 1980s. They are:

1. Develop and execute an effective system of individually guided education.

2. Provide in-service education for instructional personnel.

3. Select and test innovations before acceptance.

4. Conduct pre-service education of teachers.

5. Initiate research and development activities.[13]

In Function 1, the Research and Development Center staff coined a new name for individualizing, Individually Guided Education, so that the meaning of the concept would be clear. Too often one teacher sees individualizing as tutoring; another sees it as independent study; a third sees it as programed learning. The name and the concept of IGE were developed to provide a system for individualizing that can be understood and used efficiently.

Function 2 suggests a system for self-renewal. School staffs in the next decades must have built-in capacity for change. Statewide and systemwide in-service programs are needed. The instructional unit or the teaching team, however, is seen as the most vital organization for in-service training.

Few schools have accomplished Function 3. Too often, innovations and new materials are not tested before they are tried in the school. When I walk into an elementary school and ask, "What have you done this year that you're proud of?" someone may answer like this: "We put in the Company A phonics program." If you ask, "Is that the best program?" people become defensive. If you ask, "Is that program better than Company B's?" they become more defensive. And if you ask a technical question, such as, "Is it really better to teach vowels before consonants?" they become argumentative.

Professor Jack Frymier of Ohio State tells a story of how innovation came to one small Ohio school system. While visiting the superintendent, he asked, "What are you doing this year that you're proud of?"

The superintendent answered, "We've got modern math this year."

"Oh?" said Jack. "Tell me about it."

"Well," said the beaming superintendent, "we did everything right. We set up a textbook study committee with one teacher from each grade, and we chose the best textbook series available. But I told the salesman that I wouldn't buy the series unless he gave us some in-service training. He agreed and sent a consultant to work with us the afternoon before school started."

"How'd it go?" asked Jack.

"Not too well at first," admitted the superintendent. "I caught the teachers going back and using the old books."

"How did you stop that?" Jack asked.

The superintendent smiled, reached into his pocket, and took out a key. He said, "I got this master key to the classrooms. One night after all the teachers had gone home, I went into the rooms, gathered up all the old math books, and threw them away. Now we have a real modern math program."[14]

Each elementary school in the future should be involved in Functions 1, 2, and 3, since these are required for continuous education improvement. Functions 4 and 5 will occur in some schools. Schools may join in partnership in the pre-service education of teachers. Teaching centers have been organized around Southwest Minnesota State College and the University of Maryland, for example. Other schools may initiate or participate in research projects. The Wisconsin Research and Development Center has encouraged many schools to participate in basic and developmental research projects.[15]

IGE Begins

During the 1965-1966 school year, the first multi-unit elementary schools were organized. These schools were designed to implement IGE, and they were so successful that during the 1968-1969 school year the Wisconsin Department of Public Instruction selected the IGE model for statewide demonstration and installation.[16]

School districts throughout the United States became interested in IGE. The implementation of IGE schools was facilitated by the Institute for Development of Educational Activities, Inc. (I/D/E/A) of the Charles F. Kettering Foundation. Since 1965, I/D/E/A has given leadership for innovation that improves instruction in the schools. This group accepted the IGE school as developed by the Wisconsin Research and Development Center as a logical structure for elementary schools. The I/D/E/A staff refined the model and developed sets of in-service materials to help staffs implement IGE.[17]

The Institute for Development of Educational Activities has organized facilitating agencies throughout the United States. Each agency has provided leadership to organize cooperative leagues of IGE schools. This alliance of schools and support agencies has helped elementary schools implement IGE programs successfully. In 1971, the Wisconsin Research and Development Center received a grant from the Office of Education of the Department of Health, Education and Welfare for nationwide installation of IGE. These funds were used by state departments of education to implement IGE schools. The success of these two national movements may reflect that IGE is the first realistic alternative to the age-graded, self-contained classroom organization that has prevailed in elementary schools for so many years.

Putting Innovations Into Practice

Each of the three individualized instructional models accepts nongraded schools, team teaching, multi-age grouping, differentiated staffing, and diagnostic-prescriptive teaching, not as innovations, but as the way schools ought to be organized. So when a school staff says, "We're going to become an IGE (open, nongraded) school," they have bought an entire package.

Let us look briefly at these five ideas and the implications for school staffs considering implementation.

Nongrading

There is a story about a boy who ran to his fourth grade teacher with a bug he had found on the playground. "Teacher!" the boy cried. "Look at this bug!"

The teacher (who wasn't really too enthusiastic about bugs) said, "That's nice, Johnny."

The boy asked, "Can we study it?"

"Oh, no," the teacher replied. "That's a fifth-grade bug."

This is a ridiculous story—one that probably is not true. But it reflects the absurdity of the graded school organization.

As I pointed out earlier in this chapter, nongrading is a vertical pattern of school organization. Each student is allowed to progress through school at his own individual rate. Each student masters as much of an appropriate curriculum as he can during the year. At the beginning of the next year, he starts where he left off and again works at his own speed. No grade label is attached to work at any time. There are no promotions and no retentions. A slow-learning student may take longer to master work, but he is not "held back a year" or "pushed to keep up with the class." The academically talented student may master curriculum faster than he would in a graded school, but he does not skip material or mark time waiting for less able students to catch up with him. Ideally, the curricula are adapted to individual students so that there is no question of going faster or slower, only of using each student's abilities to best advantage.[18]

In a graded school, teachers, parents, and administrators have certain expectations for fifth-grade students, for example. The child is matched with a label on the textbooks. He is expected to learn fractions and to study the United States—even though students of the same chronological age range, in attainment, over many school grades. It is as if the school handed the fifth-grade teacher thirty sets of size ten clothes. How many children would the clothes fit? For some they would be too small; for others, too large. But in the graded school we say, "Wear the clothes. It's okay if they sag or if the shoes are tight. A little discomfort is good for children."

Just the opposite happens in the nongraded school. The teacher is asked to measure her students to find out what sizes of clothes they need. A size twelve suit with long legs. Shoes with narrow heels. Fine! No discomfort for children in the nongraded school.

Talking about nongrading is easier than changing the graded structure, however. We are so used to the graded concept that it is difficult not to use "That's third-grade work," or, "He tested 5.5" as part of our normal language. But individualized programs will not work within the graded structure. During the implementation years, IGE schools slowly change from graded to nongraded schools.

Team Teaching

If individualized instruction is truly going to affect the lives of boys and girls, it cannot be a one-teacher, self-contained program. In reading Herbert Kohl's fine book *36 Children,* you can see how one teacher's efforts did personalize an instructional program and did help each individual student function nearer to his potential. The sad part was that when the students left Kohl's classroom, they were thrown back into the group-taught, impersonal classroom to flounder or fail. Successful individualized programs require cooperation between teachers within a school and between schools in a school system.

In good schools, good teachers have always worked together. Team teaching or cooperative teaching is a logical plan for instructional organization. Robert Anderson in *Teaching in a World of Change* provides the following definition for team teaching: "Team teaching is a formal type of cooperative staff organization in which a group of teachers accepts the responsibility for planning, carrying out, and evaluating an educational program, or some major portion of a program, for an aggregate of pupils."[19]

Perhaps that definition is too formal. Somehow successful teaming occurs when "my" students become "our" students. I used to teach "Mrs. Miller's students" social studies, while she taught "my" students language arts. That's not teaming; it's trading. Mrs. Miller did not really care what I taught. I never bothered to check what she taught. The students never became "our" students.

Here is another example of a school program where teaming does not exist. Once I was standing in the hall of an elementary school talking with a teacher. A small boy came running down the hall and zoomed right past us. The teacher looked at me, shrugged her shoulders, smiled, and said, "He's not one of my students." Right then I knew that I was not in a team teaching school.

Anyone who has studied the literature on team teaching knows that there are many advantages to it. Team teaching provides (1) increased opportunities to individualize instruction; (2) better preparation and better instruction; (3) greater flexibility in grouping, scheduling, and use of space; (4) better use of the staff; and (5) greater opportunity for in-service growth of the staff.

If there are all these advantages to team teaching, why are schools primarily organized into self-contained classrooms? Teaming is not easy; it is difficult to establish effective teaching teams. Team teaching has been compared to a Chinese marriage. If marriage is difficult to keep going when one selects his own partner, consider the problem that occurs when someone else selects your partner (or partners). That is how much of teaming happens—a new teacher is guided by the principal to three other teachers who are seated together at a table. He says, "Mrs. Jones, I'd like you to meet the other members of the unit team." It's a Chinese marriage!

In 1965, the first year that I was a principal of a team teaching school, I thought that each team would break up by October. A teacher would come into my office and say, "I can't work with John," or "Evelyn makes all the decisions for our team," or "Jerry is constantly clearing his throat; I just can't stand to meet with him." I have seen personal habits, sex, politics, religion, and decision-making procedures break up teams.

Some of our Chinese marriages did not work, but since then we have all learned some ways to help teams work together effectively. There is a strategy for developing skills for team teaching. This strategy and the activities to achieve it are presented in Chapter 10.

Multi-Age Grouping

Multi-age grouping is based on two *if's:*

1. IF children learn more from other children than they do from teachers . . .

2. IF you learn more by teaching a subject than taking a subject . . .

then a child has the right to be the youngest in a room so that he can learn from older children, and he has the right to be the oldest in the room so that he can teach younger children.

Individually Guided Education uses a school organization plan that enhances multi-age grouping. The rationale for this multi-age organization includes the following points: (1) learning improves when students of varying ages are put in the same unit; (2) while individuals learn from people who are similar to themselves, they also learn from individuals who are different from themselves; and (3) since it is not possible to set one common grade level for all students in a multi-age unit, individualized instruction is a necessity.

Multi-age grouping also helps students develop positive self-concepts. It is amazing how the family group structure in the British Infant School has taught older students to be concerned about and care for the "little ones." Pairing, in which an older student serves as a model or tutor for a younger one, helps both the students' learning and their feelings about their personal worth.

Take the case of Joey and Tommy. Joey, a nine-year-old, was having difficulty learning his multiplication facts. Tommy was just starting his multiplication facts. So the teacher asked Joey if he would help Tommy. Tommy began to learn his facts. Joey began to master his facts and to feel good about himself. His statement sums up this concept: "Teacher chose me to help Tommy with his multiplication. Me! Wow! I don't multiply too well myself, but I can teach Tommy a few things. And Tommy—he's getting better at multiplication." There are many such possibilities for pairing students in a multi-age classroom.

Parents have a hard time understanding multi-age grouping. In the fine little book *IGE Multi-Age Grouping,* the story is related of the time a principal at a PTA meeting asked all the parents who were twenty-nine years old to come up to the front of the group. When they got up front, he said that he would teach them a song that they could sing at the annual PTA revue. The parents began complaining all at once.

"I can't sing."

"I can't carry a tune."

Only the soloist in the church choir seemed pleased to be up front.

"Why us?" asked one father.

"You're twenty-nine years old," explained the principal. "You ought to be able to sing a song for the group."

"Why did you choose twenty-nine year olds?" asked the father. "You must consider other factors, not just age."

"Exactly," the principal answered. "And that's what we're going to talk about tonight: why our school is planning to use multi-age grouping instead of grouping according to age."[20]

The school band is a good example of multi-age grouping. What are the criteria for being in the school band? Are all sixteen-year-olds automatically in the band? No. To be in the band a student must be able to read music, play an instrument, and march. Multi-age grouping really says that *age does not matter.*

Differentiated Staffing

Following are two lists of typical IGE units. These units are models of the way some schools have organized. Although the structure of the two units is different, both units follow the concept of differentiated staffing, which is an accepted pattern in the organization of an IGE school.

Unit A

   1   unit leader
   4   teachers
   1   clerical aide
   1   instructional aide
150   students, ages 7, 8, 9

Unit B

   1   unit leader
   3   teachers
   1   pre-service teacher
   1   volunteer parent aide
110   students, ages 7, 8, 9

Unlike some differentiated staffing programs that have created a complex hierarchy and a number of new roles and titles for personnel, the unit pattern has established only one new position—the unit leader. This is a position for the career teacher. The unit leader plans with the unit staff and coordinates the efficient use of materials and resources. She teaches 50 to 80 percent of the time. She represents the unit on the building's Instructional Improvement Committee.[21]

One idea used in the unit organization that I like is the use of the term instructional aide. This term appeals to me much more than that of a teacher aide, who by implication helps with teaching but does not perform other duties. Many communities have resisted hiring teacher aides because they believe that teachers are paid well and ought to do their own work. Maybe nursing would never have caught on as a profession if nurses had been called "doctors' helpers."

There is a need for instructional aides. Most teachers spend too much time in tasks that do not require professional competence and responsibility. They collect money, monitor recess, duplicate materials, give tests, and so forth. Such duties are a necessary part of an educational program and must be handled by someone. But paraprofessional tasks can be performed by an instructional aide under the supervision of the unit teacher. The idea of employing instructional aides to improve the quality of each student's learning program is a good one.

Diagnostic-Prescriptive Teaching

Diagnostic-prescriptive teaching is an accepted component in IGE

Fig. 5. Instructional Management Model

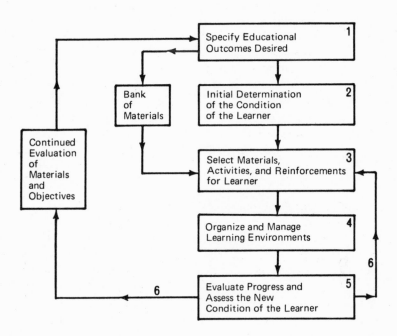

schools. Figure 5 shows the steps that a team must follow in diagnosis and prescription. (The program is explained in detail in Chapter 4.)

The Instructional Management Model has been used by the Division of Education at Southwest Minnesota State College to identify the competencies a teacher needs in a system that uses diagnostic-prescriptive teaching.

First, a teacher must know what educational outcomes or goals are desired and how to translate each of these goals into behavioral objectives.

Second, the teacher needs skills in pre-assessment. She needs to determine the initial condition of the learner. Pre-assessment is based on the idea that no student should study something that he already knows or something that he is not yet ready to learn.

Third, once it has been determined that a student does not have a certain skill but has the necessary prerequisite skills to learn it, the teacher must be able to select materials, activities, and reinforcements for the learner. This selection must take into consideration not only a student's test scores but also his learning style.

Fourth, the teacher must have skills to organize and manage learning environments so that all the students in a unit can efficiently achieve their objectives.

Fifth, the teacher must be able to evaluate the progress of a student. She must determine if the student has mastered an objective. If the student has not achieved mastery, the teacher must have the skills to recycle him to additional learning activities. If the student has achieved mastery, the teacher must have the skills to assess his new condition and to prescribe new objectives for him to study.

Components of IGE

There are four major components of the IGE school:
1. The Multi-unit Elementary School
2. The IGE Learning Cycle
3. Home-School Relationships
4. A Cooperating League of IGE Schools.

These components are discussed in other chapters of this book.

Schools exist for children. All that is done to establish and maintain schools must be measured in terms of what is best for the child.

Chapter 3
How an Individualized School Is Organized

One of the difficult tasks innovative educators have faced is the organization of an individualized program. Traditionally, elementary schools have been organized in a mass-production structure similar to the industrial plant across the river. In other words, we have adjusted the child to the curriculum instead of the curriculum to the child. The inflexible curriculum sustained grade groups and evaluation by standardized norms.

Experiences in the traditional school have made it difficult for us to envision an organization that could facilitate the teacher's role in individualizing. In an IGE multi-unit elementary school, a structure is provided so that the school staff can achieve individually guided education. It is a structure for shared decision making.

The Multi-Unit Structure

The multi-unit school system is an organizational-administrative structure designed to provide for educational and instructional decision making at appropriate levels. It provides a structure for open communication among students, teachers, and administrators.[1] When more people are involved in making decisions, the decisions tend to be better and more readily carried out.

Figure 6 shows the formal organization plan of a multi-unit program for six hundred students. This organizational hierarchy consists of three distinct levels of operation. The three levels are the unit, the Instructional Improvement Committee (IIC), and the System-Wide Policy Committee.

Fig. 6. Organizational Chart of a Multi-Unit Program for 600 Students

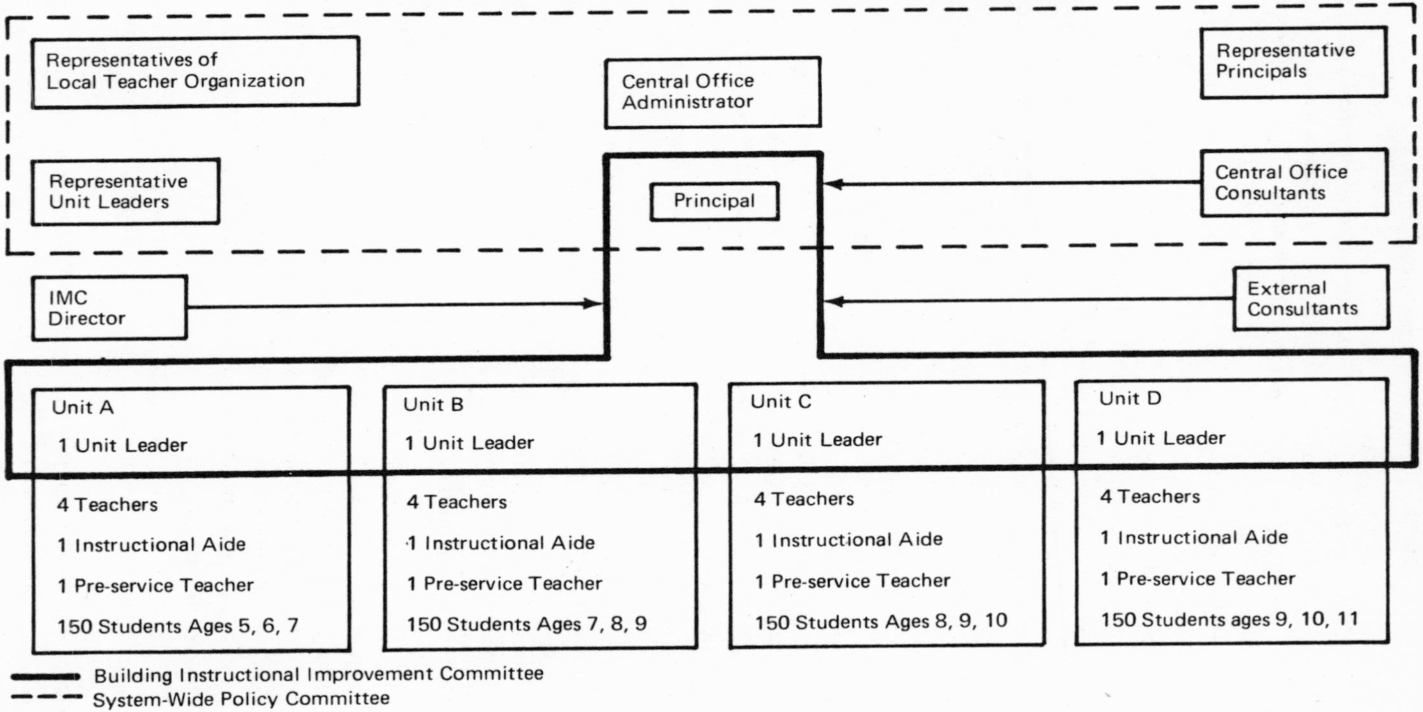

Representatives of Local Teacher Organization

Representative Unit Leaders

Representative Principals

Central Office Consultants

External Consultants

Central Office Administrator

Principal

IMC Director

Unit A
1 Unit Leader

4 Teachers
1 Instructional Aide
1 Pre-service Teacher
150 Students Ages 5, 6, 7

Unit B
1 Unit Leader

4 Teachers
1 Instructional Aide
1 Pre-service Teacher
150 Students Ages 7, 8, 9

Unit C
1 Unit Leader

4 Teachers
1 Instructional Aide
1 Pre-service Teacher
150 Students Ages 8, 9, 10

Unit D
1 Unit Leader

4 Teachers
1 Instructional Aide
1 Pre-service Teacher
150 Students ages 9, 10, 11

—— Building Instructional Improvement Committee
- - - System-Wide Policy Committee

Decisions at the unit level are made by all the people in the unit—adults and students. Each unit has a unit leader, two or more regular staff teachers, one or more instructional aides or secretaries, in some cases pre-service teachers or interns, and from seventy-five to one hundred students.

Decisions at the building level are made by the IIC, which is composed of the principal and the unit leaders. The IIC meets weekly or more frequently to facilitate school-wide decision making. The IIC is not only a decision-making body, it is the communications lifeblood of the multi-unit system. Its primary function is to move the decision-making process to the appropriate level in the hierarchy so that decisions are made by those most capable of making them. This shared decision-making process drastically changes the role of the principal from that of authoritarian administrator to that of educational leader.[2]

Decisions at the school district level are made by the System-Wide Policy Committee. This committee consists of the superintendent or other relevant central office staff, IGE principals and other representative principals, representative teachers (preferably from the local teacher organization), representative unit leaders, and consultants as needed. The System-Wide Policy Committee makes certain that the necessary materials and human resources are available for IGE and that an articulation plan between the IGE school and the junior high school is developed. Often this committee meets monthly so that IGE functions are properly interpreted to the school board and the community.[3]

Unit Staff Responsibilities

The unit staff is charged with the total education experience and instructional process of the students assigned to the unit. The assessment of each student, the development of objectives, the selection of instructional materials and activities, the placement of each student, and the means of evaluation are decided jointly. This process permits each student to benefit from the combined talents of the teachers in the unit.[4]

Planning

Planning for instruction and cooperative effort are crucial in the operation of an effective unit. At least three hours each week should be scheduled for planning, with the unit team agreeing to meet regularly. Unit meetings may be scheduled before or after school by assigning special teachers (art, music, physical education) to a unit at that time or by dismissing school early. The meetings are used for planning and evaluating the instructional program, for in-service training, and for studying student progress.[5]

The IGE planning system for developing instructional programs uses four kinds of unit meetings.

In the *Goal Setting Meeting,* the unit team selects the broad instructional goals for the unit and chooses the appropriate content to achieve these goals. One unit teacher is assigned to do preliminary research and planning for the proposed instructional program. After the Goal Setting Meeting, this teacher researches and organizes the content, reviews available instructional materials, develops teaching strategies, creates an assessment plan, and proposes a grouping strategy.

In the *Design Meeting,* the teacher presents her plan to the other unit members, who critique and modify it until it is acceptable to all. Each unit member is assigned specific tasks, and a schedule is developed. After the Design Meeting, the students are assessed.

In the *Grouping and Scheduling Meeting,* the students are grouped according to test data and other criteria. A detailed outline of instruction is developed, and the unit then begins learning activities.

While the instructional program is in process, *Situational Meetings* may be necessary to plan field trips, to reassign students or teachers, and to plan new activities.[6]

In-service Education Meetings must be scheduled regularly— monthly or more frequently. Team members must have the capacity to change and to improve the instructional program continually. A unit must be self-renewing. The unit teaches itself as members constantly learn and improve through interaction with each other. At in-service training meetings, IGE and other training materials may be studied, consultants may work with the unit, or a team member may report her findings on a topic or on a visit to another unit. A unit must never stop learning and growing and educating itself.

The meetings described above are necessary for the unit to plan, to instruct, to manage, and to improve an IGE program. More detailed descriptions of the instructional program are included in Chapters 5 and 6.

Assigning Students to Units

Each local school staff develops its own plan for assigning students to units. There are, however, some general guidelines that all schools should consider.

How many students can a unit staff "know" so that an individual learning program based on diagnosed needs and learning styles can be developed for each student? Size of the unit is important. Individually Guided Education school staffs have found that the teaching team can manage an individualized program for from 75 to 150 students. When a unit becomes larger than 150, management becomes more difficult.

How many age levels should be included in a unit? Multi-age grouping is an important element in IGE. Students of at least two age levels should be placed in a unit. Some units have age spans of three or four years. It is much more desirable to take seventy-five nine-year-olds, seventy-five ten-year-olds, and seventy-five eleven-year-olds and make two multi-age units than to put all the students of one age together.

What range of achievement should be included in each unit? Each unit should have a full representation of achievement. There is no advantage, and many disadvantages, in developing a "smart" unit and a "dumb" unit. (Many school staffs examine the achievement range of a particular age group within the unit, using standardized reading scores, and then divide students of the same achievements between two or more units.)

Are gifted students or special-education students placed in the units? Yes. Staffs of IGE schools in Wisconsin have found that a single unit can accommodate students who perform at the extreme ends of the achievement range. Some schools have found it more efficient to put all students who qualify for special education in the same unit. In this way, the special-education teacher can become a member of the unit team. Special-education students can become functioning students in the unit and can also be given special attention. When this arrangement was first used in one school, a student who had previously been in a self-contained special-education classroom told the principal, "I don't think they (the unit team and other students) know that anything is wrong with me."

How do you achieve balance in the units? In assigning students to units, the staff must consider the personal characteristics of the students.

Each unit should have some "sparklers" (students who have a positive attitude toward learning and who serve as leaders or models for other students). The staff should identify the sparklers and see that each unit has a share of them.

Each unit should have some problem students (hard to teach). These are students who have some learning disability (emotional, physical, or intellectual) that requires excessive one-to-one teacher time. If all these students are put in the same unit, it becomes a difficult situation.

Peer relationships should be considered in placing students in a unit. Students who work well together can be kept together. Students who do not work well together or who are too dependent on each other can be separated.

Student-teacher relationships must also be considered. Students who need a special kind of teacher can be placed in a unit with that kind of teacher. Whether a student works well or does not work well with a particular teacher should be considered in placement.

Age is another factor to be considered. The unit is a family. Is it better that the student be the youngest in the "family," in the middle, or the oldest?

In all cases, a balance of boys and girls should be achieved, taking into consideration achievement range, sparklers, problem students, and teacher relationships.

The delightful thing about the multi-unit elementary school is that students and parents can have a voice in the assignment problem. In the traditional elementary school, parents try to get their child into Mrs. X's class or to keep him out of Miss Y's class. Now the student's or parents' wishes can be considered. Is it better that Joey be the youngest student in the unit, since he is the oldest child in his family? Will Judy and Pam learn better together, or should they be separated? At a year-end parent conference, if a parent or teacher believes that Albert will perform better with a male teacher, he can be placed with Mr. E. There are many possibilities in the multi-unit school.

One of the early IGE schools, Wilson School in Janesville, Wisconsin, uses the following priority guidelines for establishing instructional units.[7] The basic assumption is that instructional units should be formed by looking first at the learners and then assigning the teachers to the units to meet the learners' needs.

1. Each unit should have a three-year age span, with more older than younger students.

2. Each unit should have a broad learner-achievement range.

3. Older learners with leadership ability should be placed in each unit.

4. Each unit should hold-over approximately one-half of its students.

5. Learners who do not interact well with each other should be separated.

6. Learners who require a one-to-one relationship for learning should be recognized and distributed evenly among units.

7. Learners who need structure and those who need permissiveness to learn effectively should be balanced in each instructional unit.

8. Learners who use different learning modes for success should be balanced in each instructional unit.

Assigning Teachers to Units

Individually Guided Education schools assign teachers to units in many ways. The goal of unit staff selection is building a team that has the greatest potential for planning and implementing IGE.[8] Norman Graper, principal of Wilson Elementary School in Janesville, Wisconsin, says, "As a principal of a Multiunit elementary school, you must deliberately build small decision-making societies. These societies must develop competencies in problem-solving and interpersonal relationships. The major strength of the Multiunit organization lies in these small societies and the principal's ability to function as the instructional leader in these small societies."[9]

The first decision to make when a school adopts IGE is who on the staff will stay and who will leave. It is best if a school can adopt IGE with total staff consensus. But teachers who are unwilling to participate in a unit should be allowed to transfer to other schools.[10]

The second decision is the selection of the unit leaders, which is the responsibility of the principal. There are many guidelines for selecting unit leaders. The unit leader should be properly certified and a career teacher; she should have leadership capabilities and be willing to accept extra responsibilities; she should command the respect of students, parents, and other staff members; she should believe in IGE; and she should want the job. It is suggested that the principal develop a job description for unit leaders and request formal applications. Even though a teacher fits the formal criteria for the job, the principal should consider informal criteria. Will the staff accept her? Is she skilled enough in group dynamics to keep the unit on target? Does she follow through?[11]

Once unit leaders are selected, the IIC should meet to make preliminary assignments to units. These assignments are preliminary because each teacher should be consulted to see if the assignment suits her. If not, some shifting may be necessary.[12]

Since the students in each unit represent different ages and all levels of achievement, teachers assigned to a unit should have many talents, interests, and skills. Teachers who teach in both structured and unstructured ways, as well as experienced and inexperienced teachers, should be assigned to each unit.

Some IGE schools use the teachers' subject area strengths and preferences about student age to organize units. Even though all teachers in a unit teach all subjects, the idea of having unit teachers serve as resource teachers in language arts, mathematics, science, and social studies has proven successful.

One interesting way to organize a unit team is to select members with different specific skills. The unit leader should have exceptional leadership and management skills. One unit member should be a diagnostician, with special skills for pre-assessment and prescriptive teaching. Another member should be a multimedia curriculum specialist who has the skills to develop instructional programs. A fourth team member should be a learning-process specialist who has skills in human relations, in small-group learning modes, and in educational climate development.

Obviously, the needs of the students must be considered when assigning teachers to units. It is my opinion that the worst way to organize units is to put two grades together and select the teachers of those grades to become the teaching team.

The Roles of Unit Members

The Unit Leader

The unit leader is a member of the IIC, the leader of her unit, and a teacher. As a member of the IIC, she contributes to the planning and development of the instructional program at the building level and serves as liaison between the unit staff, the principal, and other units. Within the unit, the unit leader provides leadership for developing, executing, and evaluating IGE; she coordinates the assessment program and the placement of students in appropriate learning activities; she assumes leadership in initiating, establishing, and maintaining good home-school relationships; and she teaches about three-fourths of the time. In units where pre-service education or research and development are included as goals of the elementary school, the unit leader also has responsibility for on-the-job training of intern teachers or for research and development projects.[13]

The Unit Teacher

The unit teacher's role is different from that of the self-contained-classroom teacher. She works as a member of the unit team in cooperatively planning and teaching a larger number of students than she would in a regular classroom. Team teaching tends to result in more professional levels of teaching.[14] A unit teacher's role includes the whole spectrum of instruction. She (1) selects content; (2) establishes objectives; (3) pre-assesses each student; (4) selects materials, instructional activities, and teaching strategies; (5) groups students according to pre-assessment data and learning styles; (6) evaluates student progress; and (7) provides guidance and motivation for individual students.[15]

Because she is involved with all the relevant functions of the school program, a unit teacher usually finds her new role rewarding and stimulating. One teacher, who chose to work in an IGE school her last year before retiring, said, "I wanted to make my last year my best one. Now I don't want to quit. I only wish that IGE had been available sooner in my career."

Pre-Service Teachers

Interns and student teachers can play key roles in IGE. The multi-unit elementary school offers many advantages for pre-service teacher education. In traditional, self-contained classrooms, the pre-service teacher watched, taught a little, and then took the total classroom responsibility while the regular teacher sat in the lounge drinking coffee. In the IGE school, extra hands are needed. Pre-service teachers who are "almost" professionals can assume responsibility for one-to-one teaching, small-group teaching, and other classroom activities. The pre-service teacher can develop and demonstrate those competencies that are needed and required by teachers in individualized programs. She has the advantage of being assigned to a team rather than to an individual teacher. The pre-service teacher does not have decision-making responsibilities for the instructional program as the unit leader and unit teachers do. The pre-service teacher does, however, carry out decisions and participate in unit meetings.[16]

Teacher-education institutions have found distinct learning advantages for pre-service teachers who work in IGE schools. At the same time, IGE schools have found that pre-service teachers make a tremendous contribution to the individualized instructional program. It has been a happy marriage for both.

Aides

Instructional aides and clerical aides are used in the multi-unit elementary school. Their precise responsibilities vary according to school district policy and the training and experience of each aide.

The instructional aide's responsibilities may include (1) preparing audio-visual materials and displays; (2) assisting students in seatwork assigned by the teacher; (3) setting up and operating audio-visual equipment; (4) assisting in special subjects, such as music, art, and physical education; (5) pretesting and post-testing students; (6) playing educational games with and reading to students; (7) listening to students read; (8) supervising students; and (9) helping students finish their work.[17]

The clerical aide's responsibilities may include (1) typing, (2) keeping student records, (3) collecting monies, (4) maintaining files, and (5) picking up supplies.[18] In schools where funds for aides are not available, parent volunteer aides have been used successfully. Teachers in IGE schools have found aides especially helpful.

The Role of the Principal

As the principal goes, so goes the school. Good individualized schools have good principals. A principal is never neutral; he either makes a school program better or he makes it worse.

If a principal assumes that his role is that of a benevolent father or a little dictator, the organization of the multi-unit school may not be for him. The unitized school assumes shared decision making; it assumes a democratic administration.

The IGE school principal becomes a highly involved educational leader. He serves as an objective coordinator. He facilitates the staff members' roles in implementing, maintaining, and refining an individualized instructional program. He observes and evaluates the staff, the instructional program, and the students. He is a catalyst. He is a human resource to each unit, to the students, and to the community. Each IGE principal must follow his own leadership style, but his success will depend upon how well his interpretation of this role meets the requirements of each unit in the school.[19]

In the multi-unit school, the principal provides leadership in initiating and refining the IGE system. He organizes and chairs the IIC, arranges for its meetings, and develops agenda. He is responsible for seeing that the decisions of the IIC are carried out.[20]

Team teaching affects the IGE principal's role. He should attend unit meetings on a fairly regular basis. His attendance should not be so frequent that a dependency relationship develops, but frequent enough so that problems can be caught in the early stages. The principal must support his unit leaders. Each unit leader is developing a new role for herself, and in this time of change she depends on the principal for moral, emotional, administrative, and intellectual support.

The principal must consult with individual teachers, because implementing IGE requires more planning, work, and creative problem solving. Individual teachers look to the principal for help and support.

The principal must also coordinate the staff development program. An effective IGE program keeps a system for self-improvement alive and healthy. The principal must help unit leaders manage the use of aides and evaluate their performance. Because the units become small societies, the principal must develop positive relations both between units and between a unit and special building personnel.[21]

The principal is the chief communicator in the school. It is his responsibility to establish communication channels; to send clear, concise messages; and to evaluate how successful his communications efforts are. Before implementing an individualized program, the principal should develop a communication time line. Once IGE is implemented, a communication plan for the school year should be developed and maintained. The principal should communicate the ideas of individualization, the multi-unit organization, and student progress to parents and the community and to the central office.[22]

The principal supervises and evaluates all staff. He secures appropriate instructional materials and equipment, and he uses specialized teachers and consultants to facilitate unit operation.[23]

The vast responsibilities cited only emphasize that the principal, more than anyone else in the school, has the responsibility for seeing that IGE is achieved.[24]

Mastery learning may be the key to the movement toward individualized instruction.

Chapter 4
Criterion-Referenced Assessment and Teaching

The purpose of going to school never was to go *through* school. The purpose has always been to gain an education. Yet many students go through school, each year studying the same grammar skills, for instance, but developing little or no mastery of the skills of reading, writing, and arithmetic. As a consequence, the students who develop few skills begin to lose self-respect, and each year school becomes more frustrating and more uncomfortable for them.

Many schools today are organized for yesterday. As in the past, they are still influenced by "the normal curve," and the staff believes that age and normative grouping have an important place in school organization. The staff assumes the responsibility for determining which students follow which course. Some are directed toward college preparatory programs; others are directed toward vocational training; and still others are encouraged to drop out of school.

Elementary classrooms with Jets, Jaguars, and Prairie Schooner reading groups are still common. Students are graded on the curve. It is expected that there will be A's and F's and that students will compete for marks. Norm-referenced measures are used to compare one student's performance with other students' performances. Then these data are used to make decisions about who will pass and who will fail.

But today there is a movement toward criterion-referenced tests and criterion-referenced teaching.

Criterion-referenced measures ascertain an individual's status with respect to some criterion or performance standard. The Red Cross

Lifesaving Test is an example of a criterion standard. A student does not get an A, B, C, D, or F on the test, nor does he pass the test because he is a certain age or in a certain grade. The student either passes the test, or he fails. If he fails, he tries again, until he masters the test. The advantage of criterion-referenced measures is that they can be used to make decisions about both individuals and treatments. The student who does not pass the Lifesaving Test, for example, can diagnose his deficiencies and work on them prior to a retest.

More and more elementary schools of the 1970s and the 1980s will be held accountable for educating students—not just for sorting them into categories and passing them along. It is becoming much more important that a student develop the needed skills to become an effective reader, for instance, than that he get a particular mark or be in a certain grade. Individualized instruction is one means of teaching these skills.

Using Behavioral Objectives

Teachers in individualized schools must learn to recognize, to write, and to use behavioral objectives.

Before a curriculum is translated into behavioral objectives, a teacher, the unit team, the Instructional Improvement Committee (IIC), or the school faculty must decide in general terms what that curriculum should be—what to teach. All schools operate on the basis of certain educational goals for their students. But often the instructional goals are stated in terms so broad and vague that they are not useful in the classroom; teachers do not know how to proceed with them. When objectives are sharply focused, they provide the teacher with a sense of purpose and direction and a structure for selecting materials and procedures. They provide a criterion for answering the questions "How will I know when I have taught it?" and "How will I know when a student knows?"

Let us look at how to recognize and write various kinds of behavioral objectives.*

---

*More detailed programs for recognizing and writing behavioral objectives are included in Robert F. Mager, *Preparing Instructional Objectives* (Palo Alto, Calif.: Fearon, 1962) and W. James Popham and Eva L. Baker, *Establishing Instructional Goals* (Englewood Cliffs, N.J.: Prentice-Hall, Inc., 1970).

In the Cognitive Domain

In traditional courses, the teacher must determine prerequisites: What must a learner already know to qualify for a course? Then the teacher must describe the course. By using behavioral objectives, the teacher identifies what a successful learner should be able to do at the end of the course.

Changing instructional goals to behavioral objectives is a three-step process.

First, someone decides in broad terms what is to be taught.

Second, the instructional goals are broken into component parts.

Third, the component parts are translated into behavioral objectives, or, in other words, performance objectives. For example, one of the goals of the Wisconsin Design for Reading Skill Development is to teach students to use word attack skills. The curriculum developers broke down word attack skills into component parts, such as rhyming words, consonant blends, sight vocabulary, and vowel usage. These components were then translated into forty-five behavioral objectives.

(Perhaps a few definitions are necessary: *Behavior* is any visible activity by a learner. *Terminal behavior* refers to the behavior the student should be able to demonstrate at the end of the instructional sequence; for example, solve a story problem at the conclusion of a unit on story problems. The *criterion* is the standard or test by which the terminal behavior is evaluated; for example, given a list of twenty story problems, the student should be able to solve 90 percent of the problems correctly.[1])

The scheme for constructing behavioral objectives works this way:

First, identify the terminal behavior. What should the learner be able to do to show that he has achieved an objective?

Second, define the conditions under which the behavior can be expected to occur. In determining conditions, the teacher must decide what the learner will be provided with and what he will be denied. Such phrases as "given a protractor" and "without the aid of a map" are examples of conditions.

Third, specify the criteria of acceptable performance. A good behavioral objective must state how well the learner must perform. "To solve 90 percent of the problems correctly" and "to run the one-hundred-yard dash in fourteen seconds" are examples of performance criteria.[2]

When first writing behavioral objectives, the tendency is to use words with many interpretations, such as *know, see, understand, appreciate, enjoy,* and *believe.* An objective such as "The student should be able to *grasp the significance* of the Civil War" is not behavioral. The use of words open to less interpretation, such as *speak, write, list, compare, construct,* and *solve,* makes it easier to write good behavioral objectives.

A well-stated behavioral objective is one that succeeds in communicating the teacher's intent.[3] It is written so precisely that other unit teachers can use it to identify successful learners, and all can agree on an evaluation of the learner.

The advantages of behavioral objectives are many. They provide a structure that enables the teacher to select appropriate evaluation procedures and suitable learning activities. Effectively written behavioral objectives enable a student to tell whether he is following the proper course and to focus his energy toward relevant tasks. They also provide a structure for the teacher to modify learning activities for a student who fails to meet the criteria of the objectives, an essential requirement for mastery learning.

The following behavioral objectives include terminal behavior, the conditions under which this behavior must occur, and the criteria for acceptable performance. They may be used as models for writing objectives in the cognitive domain.

> Given a list of ten words in random order in which the first two letters are the same, the student can arrange them in alphabetical order.
>
> Given a list of twenty words, the student can write antonyms for 90 percent of them.
>
> Given ten decimal subtraction problems (tenths, hundredths, thousandths, etc.), without regrouping, the student can find the difference with 80 percent accuracy.
>
> Given a list of ten books and use of the card catalog, the student can locate each of the books on the list in the school library.

Preparing behavioral objectives is a difficult, time-consuming task. Many lists of them are available, however. It is recommended that the unit team or the IIC adopt or adapt prepared lists of objectives whenever possible, such as the Wisconsin Design for Reading Skill

Development, Individually Prescribed Instruction (IPI), Individualized Mathematics System (IMS), and Program for Learning in Accordance with Needs (PLAN). The Instructional Objectives Exchange* provides sequences of objectives in almost all subjects taught in today's schools, and many publishing companies provide behavioral objectives for use with their instructional materials.

In the Psychomotor Domain

Writing objectives in the psychomotor domain is easier, because each objective has an observable behavior and the criteria for evaluation are measurable. Following are examples of behavioral objectives in the psychomotor domain.

> At a basketball goal, the learner can make ten baskets within thirty seconds.

> Given clay, glazing compound, and access to a potter's wheel and a kiln, the learner can construct a vase at least ten inches high.

In the Affective Domain

Objectives in the affective domain are difficult to write. Many teachers attempt to write them, but for the most part those they write are neither measurable nor dependent upon instruction. "The learner should choose good literature" is obviously not a measurable behavioral objective, nor is it dependent upon instruction. The learner could choose or not choose good literature—let alone read it—with or without instruction.

Measuring change is the key to writing appropriate objectives in the affective domain, and "before and after" objectives are the easiest way to measure that change.

Objectives in the affective domain can be written for an individual student or for a group of students. The following are examples.

> After instruction in taking turns at the drinking fountain, 90 percent of the students in the readiness group can take turns without teacher supervision.

*Instructional Objectives Exchange, Box 24095, Los Angeles, California 90024.

After viewing a film on "How Friends Are Made," a student can initiate a conversation with a student he has not previously met.

Assessment Before Teaching

The second step in the instructional model for individualizing instruction is assessment (*see* Figure 5, on page 23). After translating instructional goals into behavioral objectives, and before beginning instruction, the teacher must determine the initial condition of the learner; that is, which objectives he has already achieved. Once this has been done, the assessment information is used to determine the student's next learning objectives.

Assessment before teaching is necessary for two reasons:

First, no student should study something he already knows. Assessment may reveal that a student already possesses the behaviors that the teacher has as objectives. In such a case, the original objectives can be revised upward or new objectives can be selected, saving many hours of unnecessary instructional time.

Second, no student should study objectives that he is not ready to learn. Assessment may reveal that the pupil does not have the prerequisite skills necessary to achieve the objective.[4]

Time must be set aside for assessment, since an individualized teaching program can proceed only after data about the skill development characteristics of each pupil have been collected and analyzed. Assessment takes time. It takes time from the student's instructional program; it takes time for the teacher to devise procedures, to implement the procedures, and to interpret the results; it takes time for an instructional aide to administer, score, and record results.

How can you take so much time from an already full program, you may well ask. You can because although assessment *takes* time, it also, in the long run, *gives* time by guaranteeing worthwhile instruction and appropriate content for each student.[5]

Criterion-referenced tests are both different from and similar to other kinds of tests given in schools today. There are similarities between them and weekly spelling tests, for instance:

1. Each deals with specific content.
2. Each is short and used frequently.
3. Each can be used for both pretest and post-test.
4. Each has performance criteria to guide interpretations of the results.

5. With each, the student understands the procedure and his performance.

There are, however, some differences between criterion-referenced tests and weekly spelling tests:

1. The criterion-referenced test is based on objectives; spelling tests are based on lists.

2. In the criterion-referenced test, the behavioral objectives tested apply to a logically grouped class of behaviors (for example, words with diphthongs rather than a mixed group of words with a variety of spelling patterns).

3. The behavioral objectives guide the selection of assessment content, whereas the weekly spelling test is usually guided by the words studied. Every item or task on the criterion-referenced test encompasses the whole objective.

4. In the criterion-referenced test, the criterion is usually less than 100 percent. A range of 80 percent to 90 percent is typically selected for "mastery-nonmastery" to allow for imperfections in students and tests. This is a higher standard than that necessary to pass a spelling test.[6]

A teacher cannot use a standardized achievement test to obtain the information necessary to select an appropriate instructional sequence for a student. The data are too general, and only one or two items are related to each objective. Criterion-referenced tests relate student assessment directly to the behavioral objectives desired. As in the Red Cross Lifesaving Test, the student either passes the test or he fails it. If he fails, he tries again until he can pass the test; that is, meet the objectives.

There are distinct differences between standardized achievement tests and criterion-referenced tests. Figure 7 shows these differences.

Types of Criterion-Referenced Assessment

Four types of criterion-referenced assessment are frequently used in elementary schools. These are (1) paper-and-pencil tests; (2) performance tests; (3) work samples; and (4) formal observation.

Paper-and-pencil tests require formal testing conditions. Various types of test items may be used, such as completion, multiple-choice, and short answers. A number of items—the more the better—are presented to the students, and usually the test is not timed.

The advantages of paper-and-pencil tests are obvious: they can be

Fig. 7. Comparison of Two Kinds of Tests

	Standardized Achievement	Criterion-Referenced
1. Use	To compare children to norms and to rank children within a group	To determine whether a child has mastered an objective
2. Content	Wide-ranging (relatively)	Specifically focused
3. Administration	Timed; further prescribed	Usually untimed; prescription left to discretion of teacher
4. Target Group	Designated age/grade group	Any child at a given stage of progress
5. Timing	Often unrelated to instructional sequence	Related to instructional sequence

Source: Mary Quilling, "IGE/MUS-E Assessment," a speech at the IGE Regional Conference, St. Paul, Minnesota, 1972.

administered to a large group of students at the same time, and they are easy to score. But there are disadvantages: some objectives cannot be properly translated to paper and pencil, and some students perform poorly on and fear this kind of test.[7]

Performance tests require formal but individual testing conditions. In a performance test, the tasks are identified before the test, and the expected responses are written down to ensure uniform administration. The tester presents a task to a student either orally or with a stimulus object. Tasks that can be measured with performance tests include verbal responses, construction and manipulation of materials, and sequential tasks.

There are advantages to performance tests: (1) they are applicable to young children; (2) writing and reading skills can be avoided; (3) manipulative materials can be used; (4) a wide range of questions can be asked; (5) they can be administered under almost identical conditions to different students; (6) rapport between tester and student can be achieved easily; and (7) the student can get immediate feedback. The major disadvantages are that performance testing is very time consuming and may require privacy and a special testing area.[8]

Work samples are daily assignments that are done independently. A practice exercise is analyzed to ensure content validity, and appropriate items are counted to determine if the student has mastered the objective. For example, the objective might be "Given ten subtraction problems with zeros in the ones' or tens' place in the minuend, the student will be able to do the required regrouping to solve the problems with 80 percent accuracy." A work sample from an arithmetic workbook page would be analyzed, ten problems that measure the objective selected, and the student evaluated to determine if he worked at least eight of the ten problems correctly.

The advantages of work samples are that they can be collected in a normal classroom situation, large numbers can be assessed relatively easily, and the students are not test conscious. The disadvantages are that care must be taken to ensure that the student's work was done independently and that it is valid. [9]

Formal observation can be used in daily classroom sessions to assess a gamut of activities. Formal observation requires that the teacher observe and record a student's behavior in relation to a specific objective. If a teacher wants to check to see if a student reads independently, she might develop a formal checklist with items such as "Chooses books independently," "Reads on his own," and "Concentrates while reading" and observe the student during classroom or library study time. A checklist with categories such as "Frequently," "Occasionally," and "Never" can be used to record the formal observation results. By using this assessment technique, the teacher can identify those students who read independently and those who do not. [10]

The advantages of formal observation are that objectives may be assessed unobtrusively in a natural setting and that particular objectives can be measured effectively. The disadvantages are that the method is somewhat time consuming and has a lower reliability than other kinds of assessment procedures. [11]

Using Assessment for Grouping

A study of a curriculum program such as the Wisconsin Design for Reading Skill Development is helpful in understanding criterion-referenced instruction and how it is used following initial assessment. This curriculum material is designed with performance objectives and assessment materials for each objective. In word attack, for instance, there are forty-five objectives grouped into four levels—A, B, C, and D—assuming that most students will have mastered word attack skills near the end of primary school.

The following is the sequence of steps to be taken in implementing the design.

1. Administer a level test (paper-and-pencil) to all students in the unit. The last reading book a student used can help the unit team decide which level of a test a student should take.

2. Study the test results for each student to make certain that the results are valid. If the test results do not correlate with the student's previous daily performance, consider retesting.

3. Scan the test results to determine which students need to be tested at lower and higher levels. If a student tests over 80 percent on a survey test for a level, he should be tested at the next higher level. If a student tests below 80 percent, he should be retested at the next lower level.

4. Use the unit records to identify skills that need to be taught and establish priorities for teaching these skills.

5. Form skill groups, placing only students who did not pass a subtest in a skill group. (All students in any skill group study the same behavioral objectives.) Each skill group meets only twenty to thirty minutes a day, and all teachers in the unit teach the skill groups. Sometimes special teachers, such as a remedial reading teacher, are used so that there are more and smaller skill groups.

6. Provide a place (library or classroom) for the few students who passed all criterion tests for the skills. These students can work in independent study during time for skill group meetings for the next few weeks.

7. Within a skill group, provide the materials and activities best suited for teaching each student. Many diverse kinds of learning activities can be used.

8. At every skill group meeting, assess, by observation and work samples, the progress of each student. When a student appears to have grasped the skill, he can be dismissed from the group to join the independent study group. This inverted-pyramid type of group permits a teacher to start with twenty students, for instance, and progressively have fewer and fewer, enabling her to concentrate instruction on those who have trouble achieving mastery. By the end of the instructional period (two or three weeks), perhaps only eight students will remain in the skill group.

9. At the end of the time allotted for the specific instruction, reassess the performance of each student left in the group. Record the results.

10. Regroup the students in the unit to form new skill groups.[12]

The goal of an individualized learning program is to develop the uniqueness of each student.

Chapter 5
Learning Styles

Criterion-referenced instruction provides a model for individualization. The first step in the IGE Learning Cycle is a pre-assessment of each student's level of achievement in relation to the performance objectives selected by the teacher, the unit team, or the student himself. A diagnosis of the pre-assessment data helps identify objectives the student needs to master. Once this has been done, the unit team attempts to determine the kind of learning experiences that will help the student master the objectives.

In providing options for the student to master the objectives, the unit team considers both how the student will study and what materials he will use. In other words, the unit team attempts to tailor the student's learning program to fit his personal learning style.

What is learning style? Learning style in individualized instruction means those factors that ease and facilitate learning for an individual student in a given situation.[1] Does the student work best in a small group, large group, pairing, one-to-one, or independent study situation? Which sensory factors does he use best? What is his learning tempo? How does he go about solving problems?

Educational researchers have traditionally asked questions such as "Is textbook A better than textbook B?" "Is Mrs. Miller a better teacher than Mr. Dean?" "Is this new treatment better than the traditional treatment?" To answer questions such as these, average gains in achievement of students using the new treatment (inquiry, IPI, etc.) are compared with average gains for students using the old treatment. The results frequently show that there is no significant difference on the average between the two treatments. A school staff may decide not to use a new treatment because that mythical "average student" did not do better statistically.

These are the wrong questions. While the difference on the average may be negligible, there are often widely different effects on individuals.[2] For example, Pepper may respond favorably and achieve well with the new treatment; Bobby may respond favorably and achieve well with the textbook mathematics program; and Susan may not achieve at all in the traditional mathematics program.

An individualized program recognizes the fact that there is no "average student"; each is an individual who learns in his own way and in his own time. In other words, each has his own learning style. Educators who are concerned with learning styles are asking new questions, such as "Which students learned with the new treatment?" "Which students learned with the old treatment?" "Which students are placed in programs where the treatment is not effective?"

The goal of an individualized learning program is to develop the uniqueness of each student. To do this, teachers must look at the overall learning personality of each student. A study of learning styles helps a unit team accomplish this.

Assessing Learning Styles

While there are at present no formal tests for determining learning style, three systems have been devised for classifying learning styles. In considering these systems, it is suggested that the reader keep in mind the following assumptions about learning styles:

1. Each student has one or more learning styles.

2. A student should not always be placed in his best learning style; he should be encouraged to develop other learning styles.

3. When a learning task is difficult for a student, he should be placed in an activity that capitalizes on his best learning style.

4. Each student should be helped to recognize his best learning style. When this style is not appropriate (or "bombs out"), the learner should be able to use other learning styles to achieve his objective.

The staff of Wilson Elementary School in Janesville, Wisconsin, which piloted the development of IGE, has developed the following list of learning styles.[3]

Incremental Learner. This is the "bricklayer" or "blockbuilder."

He likes step-by-step learning and tends to work well on his own.

Intuitive Learner. This student "leaps to broad generalizations." Often the quality of his thinking exceeds his verbalization skill.

Sensory Specialist. This student has one predominant sense by which he learns best—by seeing, hearing, or touching. He learns from things: films, books, models, etc.

Sensory Generalist. This student uses a combination of the senses. He is over-sensitive and may need protection from too many stimuli (such as a study carrel).

Emotionally Involved Learner. This is a person-to-person learner. He needs an interpersonal relationship.

Emotionally Neutral Learner. This student has subdued interpersonal relationships. He approaches learning in a matter-of-fact method.

Eclectic Learner. This student is able to adapt himself to any learning situation.[4]

Another method of identifying learning styles has been developed by Adaia Shumsky. She states that students vary in the following ways in their approaches to and handling of a given task.[5]

Tempo in Learning. A student's individual rate of learning is often confused with his capacity to learn. A student who responds slowly may learn as much as one who reacts and absorbs quickly. Slow tempo may show cautiousness, or it may show sluggishness. Rapid reactions may signal either inaccuracies or high performance. Rate or tempo is highly individualistic. To check a student's learning tempo, the teacher may ask the following questions:

Does the student work slowly, cautiously, and accurately, or slowly and inaccurately?

Does he work quickly with good quality outcomes, or does he just complete an assignment to "get it over with"?

Does he work at a variable pace, depending on the nature of the task, or at the same speed all the time?[6]

Independence in Work. A teacher needs to know how students differ in their ability to work independently. Who are the students who can work with a minimum of teacher help or prodding? Who are the students who need help at the beginning of an assignment but can later proceed on their own? Which students need intermittent help (including those who do not ask for it)? Which students constantly need assistance? Being aware of variations in independence can help a teacher or unit team make appropriate assignments and groupings.[7]

Attentiveness. Students' attention spans vary. Some can be fully attentive for long periods of time, while others can be attentive for only short periods. Some are easily distracted. To check variations in attention, the teacher may ask the following questions:

Who are the students persistent in their capacity to attend?

Who are the highly distractable students (affected by noise, day-dreams, etc.)?

Are there students who have adequate attention in nonacademic activities and poor attention in academic activities?

Are there students who pay attention only in areas of special interest to them?[8]

Thinking and Problem-Solving Strategies. Most students have a strategy for solving problems. To check a student's strategy, the teacher may ask the following questions:

Does the student approach a learning task from beginning to end?

Does the student first overview the task and then proceed?

Does his thinking proceed from specific to general or from general to specific?

Does the student use examples of personal and concrete experiences or of nonpersonal and abstract categories?[9]

Major Learning Style. To observe a student's major learning style, the teacher may ask the following questions:

What does the student do when study time is announced?

Does he warm up for learning or starting an assignment?

How does the student make himself concentrate?

What distracts the student?

How does the student remember a story best—by hearing it, reading it, seeing and hearing it, or role-playing it?[10]

A teacher could use these questions as the basis for a one-to-one conference with a student. Such a conference would help both the teacher and the student discover the student's major learning style. The questions remind this author of his own learning style. For example, I can buy a *Playboy* magazine at the airport, read all the jokes during my flight, and not remember one of them to tell the person who meets my plane. Yet someone could tell me one of those same jokes and I would remember it clearly.

Dr. Marshall Rosenberg has identified four types of learning styles: (1) rigid-inhibited, (2) undisciplined, (3) acceptant-anxious, and (4)creative.[11] The staff of the Dayton (Ohio) City Schools has consolidated his findings as follows:

Rigid-Inhibited. This style is characterized by a student who (1) cannot get a job done without help; (2) is oblivious to what is going on in the classroom; (3) becomes confused easily; (4) misinterprets simple statements; (5) gives answers that have nothing to do with the question asked; (6) is afraid to assert himself or show initiative; (7) shows signs of nervousness (nail biting, crying, rocking); (8) is unresponsive, hard to get to know; (9) is upset by changes in routine; and (10) rigidly adheres to rules.

The teacher can help this student by (1) minimizing the ambiguity and complexity of the program (for example, presenting information in a concrete matter, reducing alternatives, keeping an easy routine); (2) adopting a supporting, acceptant attitude (providing structure for the student as he needs it); (3) insisting that the student support his statements (making him aware of what he is saying); and (4) encouraging the student to try new things.[12]

Undisciplined. This style is characterized by a student who (1) says "I can't" or "I won't"; (2) lacks tolerance for a task that he does not enjoy; (3) tends toward temper tantrums; (4) has antisocial tendencies, such as stealing, lying, destroying property, bullying, etc.; (5) speaks disrespectfully, with little trust or warmth, to the teacher; (6) blames the teacher or external circumstances when things don't go well; (7) makes derogatory remarks about the subject being taught; and (8) breaks school rules.

The teacher can help this student by (1) providing immediate feedback to the student of the social consequences of his behavior; (2) avoiding punishment but imposing immediate social consequences, such as isolation; (3) encouraging the student to slow down and to think through the cause and effect relationship of his behavior; and (4) insisting that the student support his generalizations.[13]

Acceptant-Anxious. This style is characterized by a student who (1) tries too hard; (2) shows off or tries to impress others; (3) is overly sensitive to criticism; (4) worries about pleasing others; (5) seeks teacher contact and approval; (6) is competitive and jealous; (7) tries to outdo classmates by producing more work; (8) is outwardly nervous during tests; (9) is fearful of failure; and (10) is friendly rather than distant to teachers.

The teacher can help this student by (1) minimizing the emphasis on external evaluation or rewards by permitting the learner to evaluate himself against performance standards; (2) abolishing grades or using them infrequently; (3) encouraging self-evaluation; (4) providing an environment in which the student can make mistakes without fear of ridicule; and (5) constructing situations where the student is required to think.[14]

Creative. This style is characterized by a student who (1) tells stories or describes things in an interesting fashion; (2) is open to new ideas; (3) shows persistence in attacking problems; (4) thinks creatively; (5) can extrapolate; (6) can assert himself constructively; (7) shows initiative; (8) is flexible; (9) is likely to know the material when called upon in class; and (10) shows respect for the teacher but is independent.

Teaching a student who has a creative learning style requires a flexible teacher. This learner must be provided with ample opportunity for divergent thinking and for open-ended activities. To provide for creative learners, the unit team must be creative, flexible, free to experiment, and able to allow natural curiosity and enthusiasm, to provide zest to the unit, and to spark new ideas.[15]

The teacher who recognizes the importance of learning style knows that there is not one way to learn. Students must be provided options. The whole idea of accepting students as individuals is the key to individualizing and humanizing education.

There are many more ways to think about learning styles; only a few have been described in this chapter. It is suggested that the unit team review the various learning styles, build a checklist, and informally assess the learning styles of the students in the units. Remember, a student can never be classified as having only a single learning style; each learner must be helped to recognize his best learning style and to use this style when the learning task is difficult.

Teaching Styles

Once the learning styles of the students have been assessed, the teacher must be able to accept the differences in students. Such acceptance is not easy. A teacher who accepts individual differences in students' learning styles must modify her instruction to meet these differences.

Instructional strategies can be modified to optimize learning performance.[16] This is the advantage of team teaching. A diversified team of teachers will have a variety of instructional styles, providing students with alternatives that are much more apt to match their learning styles than one teacher in a self-contained classroom can.

The staff of Wilson School has identified seven teaching styles,[17] which they use to build unit teams that can provide for different students' learning styles. The teaching styles identified are:

Task Oriented. The task oriented teacher is teacher centered; she works to get the task done.

Child Centered. With this teaching style, teaching activities emerge from the interests of the students.

Cooperative Planner. This teacher respects children. She integrates learner interest and teacher objectives.

Subject Centered. This teacher is interested in teaching a specific subject, such as mathematics, science, history, etc.

Learner Centered. This teacher is process oriented. Her teaching focuses on how the student learns.

Emotionally Involved. An interpersonal relationship develops between this teacher and the students.

Dispassionate. This teacher is emotionally neutral.

Since most teachers have only two or three teaching styles, a team of distinctly different teachers should be organized to provide for the many learning styles of the students in a unit. The idea that "'All in the Family' is all right" is a good concept.[18] Some students in a unit need a structured teacher (Archie). If a student wants answers or directions, this teacher will provide them. Some students need an open, unstructured teacher (Mike, the son-in-law). This teacher's style of teaching will encourage students who need to discover answers to do so. Some students need a warm, supportive teacher (Edith). All units need a leader. Gloria might seem a strange choice for a unit leader, but she does side with Archie sometimes and with Mike other times, and in this manner functions as a decision maker. A diversified team such as this can provide many learning options for students.*

Self-Fulfilling Prophecy

Is the "understood" child taught better? He can be. Whatever we do in teaching depends on what we think students are like. Teacher-lounge gossip can condition a unit team to expect a student to be a discipline problem. We may even behave as if an entire family is a problem: "What can you expect? He's one of the Marshall kids."

---

*A strategy for building teams is presented in Chapter 10. The plan detailed there enables a diversified group of teachers to learn to work together and avoid crises like those that occur weekly on "All in the Family."

A teacher who believes a student can learn will try to teach him. A teacher who believes a student is unable to learn may give up trying to teach him or may spend days on a treadmill, making motions that she expects will never matter.

We know that a teacher's expectation of how a student will learn often becomes a self-fulfilling prophecy. Teachers with favorable expectations of students attempt to teach much more than teachers who have unfavorable expectations do. According to Rosenthal, in experiments students who were expected to learn more did learn more.[19]

How does a teacher take advantage of the expectancy function? First, she must know the instructional objective the student needs or wants to learn. Second, she must know the student's learning styles, so that appropriate materials and activities can be selected. Finally, the teacher must have sufficient knowledge of the student's past successes and failures to distinguish between realistic and unrealistic expectancies. Past successes condition students to make realistic increases in their expectations. Past failures may condition students to lower their expectations or even never to expect success. When the teacher feels that a student can learn a task, she not only communicates that expectation, she actually tries to match instructional objectives and her teaching style to the student.[20]

The Teacher-Child Conferences for Goal Setting in *Individually Guided Motivation* are an example of this approach in action. In the goal-setting conference, the teacher encourages the student to set appropriate goals and to work to achieve the goals during the coming week. For the conferences to be successful, there must be clearly stated objectives, assessment to determine which objectives the student has not mastered, and instructional arrangements that consider the student's learning style. Research by the Wisconsin Research and Development Center has shown that goal-setting conferences are easily carried out in IGE schools.[21]

*In an individualized program, the small
group is the key instructional mode.*

Chapter 6
Learning Modes

"We know which study-skill objectives Bruce needs to learn next,"
explained the unit leader to the visitor. "We also know the ways
Bruce learns best. What we need to do is tailor an instructional
program to fit Bruce's needs and learning style."

"What does a teacher need to know and be able to do to design
and teach such a program?" asked the school visitor.

"One thing that all unit teachers must be able to do is to select
and use various learning modes," replied the unit leader.

"What's a learning mode?"

Learning modes are grouping patterns. In individualized
programs, many learning modes are used. These include (1) the one-
to-one mode, (2) the pairing mode, (3) the independent mode, (4)
the small group mode, and (5) the large group mode. By selecting a
variety of learning modes, a unit team can provide learning options
for students. Using learning modes effectively can help a unit team
tailor an instructional program for each student. This does not mean
that a student can be in the same mode all the time. It does mean
that when the student is having difficulty learning a specific objective, he can be placed in his best learning mode.

The One-to-One Mode

The one-to-one mode is used for tutoring, for the teacher to listen to
the student, and for goal-setting. For many students, the one-to-one
mode may be the most effective learning pattern. One-to-one

instruction should not be restricted to low-achieving students. All students need one-to-one instruction.

In the one-to-one mode, a student can be *tutored* to learn a new skill or to achieve a concept that he has had difficulty in mastering. All students need tutorial help. In a continuum of skill objectives, a student may have difficulty mastering a specific objective. An alert teacher will identify students who are having difficulty and provide one-to-one time for them.

The one-to-one mode provides an opportunity for the teacher to *listen* to an individual student. Book or research reports, reading conferences, and student- or teacher-initiated personal conferences are examples of the one-to-one mode in which the teacher listens to the student.

In *goal-setting* conferences, the teacher encourages the student to set appropriate goals and to work to achieve these goals within a given period of time. For effective conferences there must be clearly stated objectives, an assessment plan to determine mastery of the objectives, an instructional plan to achieve the objectives, and a specific time for a progress check and feedback.

The problem with one-to-one instruction is that a teacher may have difficulty communicating face to face with a student. There are some communication skills that a teacher can develop so that she is more effective in the one-to-one mode. For one-to-one instruction to be effective, a mutual trust must develop between the student and the teacher. It is the responsibility of the teacher to develop this relationship of trust and caring. The teacher must be aware of responses that free the student to share and those that bind or restrict the student from sharing.[1]

Responses that have a freeing effect on students include:

1. *Active, attentive listening*—responsive listening, not just silence.

2. *Paraphrasing*—restating a student's comments; this technique increases the accuracy of communication and conveys the teacher's interest in the student.

3. *Checking perception*—describing what the teacher perceives to be the student's inner state in order to check her understanding of what the student feels: "I get the impression you are angry with me; are you?" NOT "Why are you so angry with me?"

4. *Describing behavior*—reporting specific, observable actions without placing a value on them: "Bob, you've taken the opposite to everything suggested by the group." NOT "Bob, you're being stubborn."

5. *Seeking information*—asking questions directly related to what the student said, not ones that introduce new topics.

6. *Offering information relevant to the student's concerns*—the student may or may not use it.

7. *Sharing information that has influenced the teacher's feelings and viewpoints.*

8. *Directly reporting the teacher's own feelings.*

9. *Offering new alternatives*—suggesting action proposals as hypotheses to be tested.

Responses that bind or restrict a student include:

1. *Suddenly changing the subject without explanation.*

2. *Explaining the student*—interpreting a student's behavior ("You do this because your mother . . .") in a way that binds the student to the past or is seen as an effort to get him to change.

3. *Advising and persuading*—"What you should do is . . ."

4. *Denying the student's feelings*—"You have no reason to feel that way!" or a generalization: "Everyone has trouble with multiplication."

5. *Approving on personal grounds*—praising a student for thinking or acting the way the teacher wants him to act.

6. *Disapproving on personal grounds*—blaming or censuring a student for not acting the way the teacher wants him to act.

7. *Commanding*—telling the student what to do.

8. *Emotional obligations*—controlling the student by arousing feelings of shame and inferiority: "How could you do this to me?"

9. *Expectations*—can be good or bad; the teacher can bind a student to the past or she can help him achieve future goals.

These lists may seem overwhelming. The key idea to remember is that the effect of any teacher response depends directly upon the degree of trust in the relationship. The less trust, the less the freeing effect of any response; the more trust, the less the binding effect of any response.[2]

The Pairing Mode

Pairing is a variation of the one-to-one mode. In the pairing mode, two students work together on an instructional objective. For example, an older student can be paired with a younger student to serve as a tutor or a model. The younger student might be working on an objective that the older student has mastered at a minimal level. Multi-age pairing is based on the concepts that children learn more from other children than they learn from teachers and that one learns more by teaching a subject than by taking a subject. Often pairing improves the self-concept of both the older student and the younger student. Once a unit team gets to know its students, the pairing mode should be used frequently.

Another form of pairing is the study team, in which two students who are working on the same objective are encouraged to work together. Often students who have distinctly different strengths are combined as a team. For example, one might have good research skills and the other might have good art skills; a report completed by this team could be of much higher quality than two reports completed by each of them separately. In one individualized elementary school, the students indicated on a survey that they learned best while working on study teams.

Some study teams can be very stimulating and productive. Other teams may not be productive at all. The unit team should identify those students who work well together and those students who should be separated.

The Independent Mode

In the independent mode, the student works more or less alone. He interacts with materials at his own rate. The independent mode can be used when the teacher selects both the performance objectives and the media to achieve the objectives. Individually Prescribed Instruction (IPI) is an example of this mode. The objectives that the student is to master and the media to achieve them are identified through a pretest. Programed learning is another example of the independent mode in which both the objectives and the materials are selected by the teacher.

The independent mode can also be used for self-directed learning, in which the teacher selects the objective and the student selects the media that he will use to achieve it. For example, a student who is to learn to use the Dewey Decimal System may choose to read, to view a filmstrip, or to visit the library.

This mode is also appropriate in a personalized program, in which the student chooses his objectives and the teacher chooses the media. For example, if a student says that he wants to find out how the streets in the city were named, the teacher says, "That's a good project. Here's how you do it."

The independent mode can also be used for independent study.

We have found that independent study means different things to different people. In this book, we will use the term independent study as meaning that a student is permitted to select both his own learning objectives and his achievement method. Not only students who are high achievers should be permitted to initiate independent study projects. All students should be encouraged and given the opportunity to participate in independent study.

The independent mode requires the teacher to guide the student during unstructured time. The teacher should check the student's progress and his ability to use the mode.

It must be pointed out that some students do not learn well using only the independent mode. This mode can be a very "lonely" way for a student to achieve his learning objectives, and it should not be overused.

The Small Group Mode

In an individualized program, the small group is the key instructional mode. In IGE, the small group mode is the instructional grouping that is used most frequently. The reason for this is that through the years elementary teachers have been most effective while working with small groups.

The small group mode is important because it is an efficient grouping for achieving instructional goals. The group is small enough so that the individual student's interests and learning style can survive; yet it is large enough so that other students can provide spark and stimulation.[3]

This mode is efficient because (1) the teacher can give individual attention to a student's learning needs; (2) the student can become actively involved in his own learning; and (3) the small group provides for developing student leadership and for teaching the skills of discussion and group processes.[4]

Remember that the small group is a multi-age group of students (usually from four to thirteen students) who are studying the same behavioral objective. Once the objective has been achieved, the group disbands and new groups are formed.

There are many kinds of small groups. Each different small group has a specific function. The work of Allan A. Glatthorn in identifying the small group models[5] has provided leadership for teaching this mode. The author has worked with a team to develop video tapes of various small group models to instruct pre-service and in-service teachers on teaching small groups.*

The models described in this chapter have proven to be effective for instructing students in individualized programs. A step-by-step description of the teacher's responsibility is included as a guide for teaching each kind of small group.

The Skill Development Small Group†

Good teachers have always used the small group to teach skill subjects. The skill development small group is used when a number of students are studying the same skill objective. It is especially appropriate in reading, arithmetic, and study skills. It is designed so that the teacher can give the student intensive study of a specific skill.

There are seven steps that the teacher follows in teaching a skill development group (the first three steps are completed before the teacher meets with the students). The steps are as follows:

1. *The behavioral objectives in the skill area are identified.*

2. *Pre-assessment.* Students are pretested on a group of the skill objectives.

3. *The group is formed.* Those students who have not mastered the objectives but who have the necessary prerequisite skills to achieve the objective are identified. A group of from four to thirteen students is formed, and a teacher is assigned to the group. She reviews the skill and gathers a variety of materials and strategies that can be used to teach the skill.

4. *Perceived purpose and informal pre-assessment.* At the first meeting with students, the teacher explains the purpose of the skill development group and why the students are in the group. She then reviews the skill with the group, permitting them to practice the components of the skill (orally, at the chalkboard, etc.). During this review, she pre-assesses each member of the group informally.

5. *Prescription.* After the class period, the teacher uses the data

*Lowell Tornquist, Director of the Center for Applied Instruction at Southwest Minnesota State College, led the team that conceptualized, developed, or refined many of the models presented in this chapter.

†The skill development small group was developed by the author and has been field-tested in the IGE League Schools in Minnesota and in the Teacher Education Program at Southwest Minnesota State College.

she has collected to write a prescription for each student. She studies the pre-assessment test results, the student's permanent record (noting past performance and best learning style), and the informal pre-assessment. She writes an initial prescription for each student. The prescriptions may divide the students into a number of sub-groups.

6. *Diversified learning activities.* This is the most exciting and flexible part of the skill development group. The teaching area should be filled with materials and learning options for students. These include:

- a. tutorial groups
- b. practice materials
- c. pairing and study teams
- d. independent activities, such as reading materials, manipulative materials, audio-visual materials, learning stations, etc.
- e. games

7. *Post-assessment.* When the teacher has determined that a student has mastered the skill, the student should be given a post-test. If the student passes the post-test, he should be released from the group to study a new objective or for independent study. At the end of a specific time previously determined as reasonable for students to master the skill (many teams use two weeks), all students should be given the post-test. If a student has not mastered the skill, he should be recycled to study the same skill at a later date. It is probably best if the student is not recycled in the same skill immediately.

Figure 8 shows how a skill development group works. The instructional pattern in this group resembles an inverted pyramid. From four to thirteen students are initially assigned to the group. As soon as a student masters the skill, he is released for independent study or to study other objectives. The group keeps becoming smaller and smaller, so that the teacher works with only those students who need help with the skill.

The staffs of the individualized schools where this model has been used have found that it is preferable for a teacher to be responsible for two skill development groups of from four to thirteen students than for one large group (from twenty to thirty-five students). To provide more options, many schools schedule remedial or supplemental teachers and instructional aides into the unit during the block of time when the skill groups are taught.

Fig. 8. The Skill Development Small Group

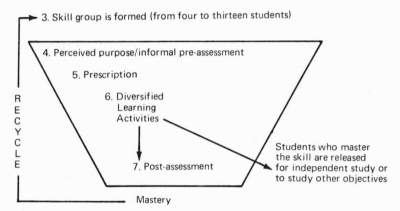

1. Behavioral objectives in the skill area are identified

2. Pre-assessment

3. Skill group is formed (from four to thirteen students)

4. Perceived purpose/informal pre-assessment

5. Prescription

6. Diversified Learning Activities

7. Post-assessment

R E C Y C L E

Students who master the skill are released for independent study or to study other objectives

Mastery

The Brainstorming Small Group

The brainstorming small group is group process for problem solving. It is based on the idea that many heads are better than one. Brainstorming is a free-wheeling method of generating solutions to an open-ended problem quickly.

The brainstorming group is carefully structured. Four "Ground Rules for Brainstorming" must be followed during the brainstorming process. One, *no criticism or evaluation* (a critic can destroy the creativity of brainstorming; criticism must be held until later). Two, *quantity of ideas is encouraged* (the more ideas generated, the more the likelihood of good solutions). Three, *the wilder the idea, the better* (creative solutions are encouraged). Four, *hitchhiking an idea is permissible* (participants are encouraged to combine and improve other ideas).

Following are the steps in brainstorming:

1. *Setting the stage.* The teacher should explain to the group how brainstorming works.

2. *Explaining the ground rules.* The ground rules should be written on the chalkboard and explained to the students.

3. *Choosing a recorder.* The ideas suggested by the students should be written on the chalkboard. Seeing the ideas helps students

generate more ideas. The recorder should be a student who can write quickly and accurately. With younger children, the teacher must serve as the recorder.

4. *Introducing a topic.* Note that the topic is not introduced until step 4. If this sequence is not followed, students will start brainstorming before they understand the process.

5. *Brainstorming process and refocusing.* Ideas are generated. If the group goes off on a tangent, the teacher refocuses the group.

6. *Evaluating.* Ideas are combined, grouped, or ranked. Some are eliminated. This step is difficult with younger children because they will want to keep brainstorming rather than evaluate. Sometimes a break should be taken between steps 5 and 6.

7. *Summarizing.* The best solutions are selected and plans are made to implement them.

The Task Small Group

The task small group is also called the committee. All of us have been on committees that met and met but did not accomplish the specific task they were assigned to do. The task group is student led, with seven clearly defined steps. The group works over several sessions, usually outside of the classroom, to solve a problem, to undertake an investigation, or to complete a project.

The steps in the task group follow:

1. *Defining the task.* The task is clearly defined. For example, "What are the pollution problems in our community?" or "How should we decorate the learning center for Halloween?"

2. *Determining individual roles.* A leader is selected. Duties for other committee members are assigned.

3. *Identifying resources.* The teacher identifies resources the group can use and those that are unobtainable.

4. *Selecting reporting procedures.* The type of feedback the committee will make to the class or unit is identified (written report, oral report, demonstration, slide presentation, etc.).

5. *Setting a timetable.* A calendar for completing the task is determined.

6. *Monitoring the data search.* In the task group, the teacher functions as a resource person rather than as an instructor or leader. However, some monitoring checkpoints (such as a visit with student leaders) should be set during the data search.

7. *Reporting.* The task group reports back its findings.

The Workshop Small Group

The workshop small group is similar to the task group, except that it takes place in the classroom under the supervision of the teacher. Examples of workshops are small groups of students painting a mural, building a stage set, or doing a science experiment. A writing workshop, in which students write lead paragraphs for news articles, pass them to other group members, read them, talk about them, and prepare them for the school paper, is another form of the workshop group. A teacher can work with a number of workshop groups at the same time.

The steps in the workshop group are as follows (steps 1 and 2 are often completed by the teacher before the class period starts):

1. *Defining the task.*
2. *Gathering resources.*
3. *Defining the task for the group.*
4. *Selecting roles.*
5. *Completing the task.*
6. *Conclusion.*

The Inquiry Small Group

The purpose of the inquiry small group is to teach students the art of asking questions to solve problems. Rather than telling the students the answers, the teacher encourages the students to ask questions and to discover the solution themselves. There are many models for inquiry. The Suchman model[6] has the following steps:

1. *Build a responsive environment.* The teacher explains the inquiry process to the students. Simply, the teacher tells the students that she will answer their questions "Yes," "No," or "Is that your theory?" She provides an environment where each learner can be heard and understood and can obtain the data he requires.

2. *Give a problem.* Suchman uses a film of a physical event as the problem. In one film, a teacher heats a metal bar over a Bunsen burner. The bar bends upward when heated. The teacher dips the bar in water and it returns to its original shape. She turns the bar over and heats it again. The bar bends downward. The film ends. The classroom teacher asks the group, "Why?"

3. *Questioning by students.* The students question the teacher for the data they require to solve the problem.

4. *Formulation of hypothesis.* A student forms a hypothesis.

5. *Testing the hypothesis.* Using the "yes-no" questions, the student tests the hypothesis.

Inquiry can be one of the most exciting small group models, but it requires a patient teacher. How many teachers could permit the inquiry process to go on for three class periods without telling the students that the bar was a bi-metal one? To see a science class end with the comment, "Well, you didn't discover what's inside a battery today; we'll work on it tomorrow," is still an unusual happening.

Another form of inquiry is teacher-directed discovery. Problems such as "How is a number related to its exponent?" permit students to work out plans. "Yes-no" questions are still used, but the teacher may lead the group by saying, "Does that work with decimal numbers?" Or, in the science inquiry group, "What's inside your mouth?" After the students have identified that the mouth and nose are connected, the teacher may ask, "Can you drink water while you're standing on your head?"

A third inquiry group works without the teacher. For example, the students are given a metal box containing forty pennies. The teacher instructs the group, "Pretend that it is two thousand years from now. You are walking down the beach and you find this box of objects. Study the objects (coins). What do you know for certain about the people who made and used these objects? What would you speculate? What questions would you like to ask them?" The group selects a recorder and works to answer the questions. This inquiry plan will work with kitchen utensils, a diary, etc.

Following this same pattern, a group is given an aerial map of a large U.S. city. There are no markings on the map. The group is instructed to locate the city and name it if they can. It's amazing how well students do on this activity.

Using manipulative objectives is another form of inquiry. For example, students are given batteries, bulbs, and wires. The teacher instructs them to find out how many ways they can place the battery, bulb, and wire to make the bulb light. Students draw a diagram of each system that works so that they can later demonstrate it to a teacher, an aide, or another student.

The Study Small Group

The study small group is a structured discussion group in which students who have read the same book or seen the same film or play can discuss it in depth. Perhaps the study group is popular because oral book reports have been so deadly. (Many teachers—and students—have hated to listen to students give book reports.)

The discussion in the study group is structured according to Bloom's taxonomy. The questions move from knowledge to application. The steps in the study group are listed below (steps 1, 2, and 3 are completed before the discussion is started).

1. *Selection of topic.* All students read the same book or see the same film or play.

2. *Identification of members.* Those students who agree to read the book or attend the movie or play are identified.

3. *Gathering information.* Time is set aside for reading or viewing.

4. *Group interaction.*

   a. *Facts.* The teacher asks the group, "What did the work say?" The facts are gathered. The story is retold. When sufficient facts are gathered, the teacher leads the group to part b.

   b. *Interpretation.* What does it mean? The teacher gives the group time to interpret what the facts mean. Some of the big ideas are identified. These are discussed in part c.

   c. *Evaluation.* One of the ideas from the work is focused on. The teacher asks the group, "Do you agree or disagree with this idea?" Evaluation of the ideas usually produces a lively discussion. Once the teacher feels that the group has adequately evaluated the ideas, she moves to the final part, part d.

   d. *Application.* The teacher asks, "Now that you've read (seen) this work and discussed it, how will it affect your life?" This part of the study group opens the discussion to higher levels than any book reports or bull sessions that we have ever seen.

The Socratic Small Group

The Socratic small group is an effective technique for presenting both sides of a controversial issue. This can be one of the most stimulating of the small groups, but it should only be used with upper elementary or older students, and even then not too frequently. Socratic teaching may require the teacher to use a teaching style quite different from her own. The Socratic group is highly structured, and the steps should be followed carefully. (Remember, Socrates was given the hemlock as his reward for teaching).

Once, with a group of in-service teachers, an instructor posed the following problem. "Our school librarian wants to eat with the rest of the school staff. The students want the library open during the noon hour. Some of the older students volunteered to keep it open. Do you think that a sixth grader is responsible enough to keep the library open during the noon hour?" One teacher immediately agreed that a sixth grader is responsible enough. The instructor began to probe, to question, to press, and to challenge the teacher's responses. The abrupt change in the instructor's teaching style and the sudden defensiveness of the teacher caused the entire group to attack the instructor. He did a lot of squirming to explain that he was demonstrating Socratic teaching.

The steps to be followed in the Socratic group are:

1. *Controversial issue is presented.* The topic must be one about which there is a difference of opinion. The teacher presents the issue clearly. She quizzes the students to make sure they understand the issue.

2. *Student commitment to a position.* Each student must commit himself. It is best if the commitment is made in writing.

3. *Intensive questioning of value conflicts.* The teacher asks the student to justify his position. The teacher appears to accept the student's justification, and verbalizes a social value that supports the position. Then the teacher presents an analogy that illustrates the other value involved in the case. It is good if the teacher can get the other students into questioning roles also.

4. *Reconsideration of position.* The student is asked to reconsider his position. If he changes or does not change, he is asked to explain his value inconsistencies. The teacher questions many of the students in the group in this fashion.

5. *Analytical study of value inconsistencies.* The teacher suspends the intensive Socratic dialogue and asks the students to analyze the dilemma.

The Discursive Small Group

The discursive, or discussion, small group provides an opportunity for a free and uninhibited discussion of a topic of prime importance to the students. The topic can be either a life experience or a value. This group is unstructured. The discursive group is an excellent means of helping students gain confidence in discussion skills. There is a danger of overuse, of the group becoming a bull session where uninformed participants "pool their ignorance." Careful teacher observation can help to keep the discursive small group productive. The teacher's role is normally that of an interested observer. However, sometimes the teacher must refocus the group when the discussion gets off the subject.

The steps in the discursive group are:

1. *Adjusting to participants.* This is a warm-up activity, in which the group begins talking about any subject so that they become accustomed to discussing topics with each other.

2. *Introducing the topic.* The introduction may be made by the teacher or by a group member.

3. *Discussion.* The group members interact with each other while the teacher serves as an interested observer. If the teacher finds the group dependent on her, she should move her chair out of the discussion circle, thus nonverbally communicating to the members, "It's your discussion!" If the discussion gets off the subject, the teacher refocuses the group by restating the topic or asking a question.

4. *Summarization.* Summarizing the discussion points is the final step.

The Role-Playing Small Group

In the role-playing small group, students assume roles to achieve a better understanding of a problem. Role playing may vary greatly. Students can assume roles and dramatize a story from reading. In social science, for example, students can be assigned specific roles to help them understand how pioneers felt when they decided to go west. For example, the father wants to go; he does not like working in the East Coast factory and he has heard how good the Minnesota farmland is. The mother is afraid to go; she has heard tales of the Indians and of the fierceness of the Minnesota winter. The ten-year-old son is excited about going. The fifteen-year-old daughter has a boy friend whom she hates to leave. The scene is set at the family meal during which the family decides to go or not to go.

In science, role playing can be used to dramatize the movement of the planets. On the playground or in the gym, one student can be the sun, another Venus, another the earth, etc., and demonstrate how the planets revolve around the sun.

Real school problems can also be studied in role-playing situations. One student can play the principal, another a teacher, another a student, etc., working to solve a current school problem.

The steps in role playing are:

1. *Introduction to role playing.* The purpose of role playing is explained to the group.

2. *Introduction of the topic.* The problem to be dramatized is introduced to the students.

3. *Selection of roles.* Student roles are assigned. These roles may be assigned within the group or to each student individually. Note that role playing should be explained and the topic introduced before the roles are selected.

4. *Setting the stage.* Furniture is arranged to help the students enact the role-playing situation.

5. *Enactment.* The teacher prepares the audience to observe. Enactment takes place. There may be some discussion and then further enactment.

6. *Discussion, evaluation of feelings and content.* The teacher provides leadership for this final step. Each student explains why he played the role the way he did and how he felt while playing the role.

The nine different small group models introduced in this chapter can help teachers and unit teams provide a structure for individualizing the instructional program.

The Large Group Mode

Schools that have had individualized instruction programs for some time have found limited use for the large group, or presentation, mode. This is quite embarrassing for some schools, because space was provided for large group presentations and now this space goes mainly unused. There are times, however, when the large group is an effective learning mode.

A large group can be an efficient way to (1) introduce an instructional unit; (2) present audio-visual materials, especially 16mm films that the school has for only a limited period of time; (3) permit a resource person to work with the students in the unit; and (4) provide for culminating activities.

As an example of effective use of the large group mode, let me share how one unit team introduced a new instructional unit.

In this multi-unit school, Unit IV was composed of eighty students who were ten, eleven, and twelve years old; three teachers; and a part-time instructional aide. From 9:30 to 10:15 each morning, the students went to special studies (physical education, art, music, and Spanish), and the unit team held a planning session. There were four other units in the school, all with similar schedules.

One morning at 9:15, the principal spoke over the public address system to the classrooms that housed Unit IV. He said, "Boys and girls, last night at the Board of Education meeting a study was presented about the use of special teachers in the elementary school. There is concern that special teachers are overscheduled. Each school has been instructed to cut the schedule of special teachers. We have studied student progress in physical education, art, music, and Spanish, and have found that Unit IV has made the best progress. We decided that it would hurt you students the least to have these subjects canceled. So, until further notice, Unit IV will have no physical education, art, music, or Spanish."

The P.A. clicked off. The rooms were in silence. Someone muttered, "He can't do it." The announcement had come just before boys' physical education. The boys who had been holding their gym shoes now placed them under their desks.

One teacher said, "We don't like this idea. There goes our coffee break and our team planning period."

The teachers gave the students a rest break. The custodian met the students in the hall and said, "Boy, I certainly think you kids got a raw deal!" In the boys' locker room, the physical education instructor told the boys that he was sorry that he would not have them in class anymore and hoped that they would remember some of the skills he had taught them.

The students were upset. They grumbled and complained to each other. When they got back to the room, one student made a sign showing the hanging of the principal. Passing it around cheered the students momentarily.

The teachers returned to the classroom and quieted the students, and the remainder of the morning went as usual.

At lunch, the students didn't play on the playground. They gathered in small groups, discussing and complaining about the ruling.

Some students had gone home for lunch, and the school office phone began to ring. The principal told the callers only, "It's an educational experiment. It won't be a problem in a few hours."

After the lunch hour, all the students in Unit IV went to the all-purpose room for a large-group presentation of a new instructional unit on the Revolutionary War.

A filmstrip projector and a microphone were set up, but before the teachers could begin the large group lesson, the principal interrupted on the P.A., "Would all the teachers in Unit IV please report to the office." The teachers left the room.

Here were eighty students in an all-purpose room without teacher supervision (they thought) and with a live mike in the front of the room. The students made noise, moved around, and threw some paper wads. Finally one boy went up to the mike and got the group's attention. "I think that we're going about everything wrong," he said. "We've complained to each other, we've made signs, we've gotten mad. But we haven't told anyone who counts that we don't like the decision. I think we should write the superintendent a letter or go and see him."

The students agreed. The boy who had spoken and two others volunteered to go to the superintendent's office after school.

Then the teachers came back in the room, quieted the group, and started the filmstrip, *Background of the American Revolution*. The team leader showed the filmstrip without comment until he came to the section where laws were made for the American colonists by the British. There, he flipped off the projector and asked, "Has anyone ever made a rule or law that has affected your lives without giving you representation in the making of this rule?"

The students began to understand what had happened to them. Questions came from all over the group. The teachers explained that they had tried to give the students a chance to know how the colonists felt. Before long, everyone in town knew that Unit IV was studying the American Revolution.

This is an example of how a large group can be used dramatically to present a unit. Another time, an instructional unit on Australia began with Aborigine drums beating in a darkened room.

Films and resource people are obvious ways to use the large-group mode. It is also an efficient mode for some kinds of testing and for culminating a unit. Panel discussions, dramatic skits and presentations, illustrated reports, displays, and debates have all been used effectively as culminating activities.

In planning individualized programs, remember that the large group mode should not be used frequently. When it is used, it should be carefully planned.

*Individualized instruction is a way of
organizing that permits and encourages each
learner to progress at a pace and level
commensurate with his unique combination
of abilities, interests, needs, and learning
style.*

Chapter 7
Using Diversified
Learning Materials

"We've become a 'ditto' school," complained the teacher. "Individualized instruction can't mean that everyone sits at his desk working with his own ditto sheet."

"You told me that my son learns best with audio-visual materials," complained the parent. "Why don't you use those materials to teach Bobby multiplication? He's not making any progress with those workbooks."

"We've individualized our math program," complained the principal. "All the kids go through the math textbooks at their own speed. But the parents say that the teachers aren't teaching and that the kids aren't learning."

In individualizing instruction, there is a danger of overusing one kind of material, or of forgetting that Bobby's best learning style has been identified, or of thinking that a particular textbook is self-teaching. The teacher in an individualized school program must be able to select and use diversified instructional materials to help the student achieve his learning objective efficiently.

In teaching a specific objective, there may be several different practice activities that are appropriate. *Equivalent activities* are those in which the student actually practices the desired terminal behavior. For example, if the objective is to add unlike fractions, the student is given practice problems and he adds unlike fractions. *Analogous activities* are those similar to but not identical to the desired terminal behavior. With the objective mentioned, the student might use Cuisennaire rods to add unlike fractions. An *enroute task* is one of a set of tasks that a student must master before achieving the terminal behavior.[1]

For each objective, the teacher must decide how many and what kind of learning options to provide. A study of materials that are used in individualized schools and the ways school staffs have developed or adapted these materials can help the teacher provide learning options for students.

Programs for Determining Objectives and Media

Individualized instructional programs vary according to whether the school or the student selects the objectives and the media. Four distinct kinds of programs are illustrated in Figure 9. These four programs can be described briefly as follows.[2]

A. *Individually Diagnosed and Prescribed Instruction.* The school determines what and how the student will be taught, setting the objectives and selecting the materials. The student is permitted to learn at his own pace.

B. *Self-Directed Instruction.* The school determines the learning objectives; the student selects the materials and decides how he will master the objectives.

C. *Personalized Instruction.* The student selects the objective; the school determines the media. Once the student has selected the

Fig. 9. Kinds of Individualized Instruction Programs

OBJECTIVES

	School Determined	Learner Selected
MEDIA — School Determined	A. INDIVIDUALLY DIAGNOSED AND PRESCRIBED	C. PERSONALIZED
MEDIA — Learner Selected	B. SELF-DIRECTED	D. INDEPENDENT STUDY

Source: *Individualized Instruction: Its Nature and Effects,* a filmstrip distributed by the Association for Educational Communications & Technology. 1970.

objective, he is required to follow an instructional sequence and use specific materials selected by the teacher. For example, the student says, "I want to study pollution in our town," and the teacher says, "Here's how you will do it."

D. *Independent Study.* The student determines his own learning objectives and selects the methods to achieve them.

Most individualized programs fit in Box A; both the objectives and the means for achieving them are predetermined for the student by the teacher. The individualized program should be structured so that students can participate in all four kinds of instruction. As a student becomes more self-directed and independent, he should be allowed to select his own learning objectives more frequently.

Skill Curriculum vs. Content Curriculum

The curriculum of the elementary school consists of two parts: skills and content. The skill disciplines include the 3 R's plus physical, manipulative, and sensory skills. The content disciplines include social studies, the humanities, and the sciences.[3]

There are distinct differences in the ways skill disciplines and content disciplines are structured. Skill subjects have a sequence or continuum of performance objectives, ranging from easy to difficult. A student starts where he is and moves through the continuum at his own learning rate. For example, the Tipp City (Ohio) math program is made up of continuous progress levels, ranging from number readiness to algebra. Skill subjects can also be organized into systematic instructional packages, such as Individually Prescribed Instruction (IPI) or the Wisconsin Design for Reading Skill Development.

Content subjects do not have sequential performance objectives. In social studies, for example, it is not important which a student studies first, Mexico or Canada. Instead, content subjects are structured—by the teacher, the unit team, or the student himself—with a dynamic interplay of facts, methodologies, and concepts.[4] Frequently, content subjects are organized into units, out of which grow meaningful individual or group projects.[5]

The student may view reading, writing, and arithmetic as skill-getting subjects, and literature, social studies, and science as skill-using subjects. In the content disciplines, he uses his skills to generate knowledge to meet his learning needs.[6] The idea of skill-getting as contrasted with skill-using may be a helpful concept for the unit team to keep in mind as they select or develop instructional materials.

Continuous Progress Skill Programs

Writing and sequencing behavioral objectives, writing and testing assessment instruments, and selecting appropriate instructional materials are difficult, time-consuming tasks. Teachers, unit teams, and Instructional Improvement Committees should not try to "discover the wheel." The teacher, unit team, or school should study continuous progress curriculum programs that have been developed by educational research agencies, commercial publishing companies, or innovative school districts before they attempt to develop their own such programs.

The components of a good continuous progress skill curriculum parallel the teacher competencies discussed in Chapter 2 (*see* Figure 5, on page 23). These components are: (1) clear instructional goals that have been translated into a sequence of behavioral objectives; (2) a system to pre-assess the initial condition of the learner in relation to the behavioral objectives; (3) a collection of or suggested list of diversified learning materials and activities that can be used to teach each objective; (4) a system for managing a student's progress in the skill objective continuum; and (5) a system to post-assess a student's progress to determine if he has mastered the objectives.

Continuous progress skill programs that have these five components can be adapted to fit local needs. The sequence of objectives can be altered. Prior knowledge of each student can be added to pre-assessment. Resource files of commercial materials and teacher-made materials can be developed for each instructional objective.

The Teacher's Resource File

In a continuous progress skill curriculum, a Teacher's Resource File for each skill to be taught should be developed. The purpose of the file is to provide teachers with a source of ideas for instructional materials. This collection of materials facilitates the teacher's role in planning individualized programs for each student in a group.

The file folder contains:

1. The behavioral objective(s) to be taught.

2. A list of materials (type, title, publisher, and page numbers) that can be used to achieve the objective.

3. Teacher-directed activities, in the form of a list of suggestions for individualizing. These would include group practice, individual practice, and manipulative aids.

4. Performance tests. (The pretests and post-tests may be filed elsewhere.)*

School staffs have found that building such a file is a good in-service activity for teachers. The process of matching materials to behavioral objectives helps teachers to understand the skill curriculum better and to identify deficiencies in the school's instructional materials.

Content Units

The most exciting teaching a unit team can plan and execute is the content unit. In Chapter 6, the beginning of a content unit on the American Revolution was described. Most content units are based on social studies, science, or literature, and many are interdisciplinary.

The author has seen exciting content units on a wide variety of topics: "Families Around the World"; "Indians—The Difference between the Sioux and the Chippewa"; "Are Snowmobiles Good or Bad?"; "Mass Product—An Experiment"; "The Renoir Room"; and many more. A creative unit team can design a content unit that helps students master facts, methodologies, and concepts in such a way that "everyone knew Unit IV was studying the American Revolution."

Writing a Content Unit

To write a content unit, the teacher (or unit team) must first decide what is to be taught. If possible, the main idea of the content unit should be written in one complete sentence. Next, this idea should be broken into component parts. Each component part should then be converted into behavioral objectives.

Note that deciding what to teach and breaking the main idea into component parts should precede the writing of behavioral objectives. Unless the writer thinks in criterion-referenced terms, starting with behavioral objectives may be limiting. Too often, teachers focus on

*A more complete description is shown in the sound filmstrip *Teacher's Resource File* (Madison, Wis.: Wisconsin Research and Development Center for Cognitive Learning, 1971).

the question "What should I do?" rather than "What do I want the students to learn and how will I know that the student knows the main idea of the content unit?"

Step One in writing a content unit, therefore, is the development of precise behavioral objectives designed to achieve the component parts of the main idea of the unit.

Step Two is the pretest. Each student should be checked to determine that he has the necessary prerequisite skills to achieve the objectives and to see if he has already mastered any of them. A pretest should contain items on each objective and on prerequisite skills.

Step Three is an outline or sketch of the day-by-day activities that will occur in the unit. This is a much less detailed description than a lesson plan, which the teacher may also choose to develop.

Step Four is a criterion check. To avoid teaching a content unit for three weeks and then having all the students fail to pass the post-test, the teacher should check three or four students to see if they are achieving the objectives. This sampling helps the teacher determine whether reteaching is required.

Step Five is a list of diversified instructional resources that will be used to achieve each objective of the unit.

Step Six is the post-test. The post-test should include items on each behavioral objective in the content unit. Both the pretest and the post-test can consist of any kind of assessment; they should not be limited to paper and pencil items.*

Teaching a Content Unit

Content units are taught in an "umbrella" fashion. For example, all the students in a unit study under the umbrella of the topic "The American Revolution." The students' programs, however, are individualized. Students have different objectives and use different materials and activities; some study the subject in much greater depth than others.

Multi-age grouping affects the way a content unit is taught. Since the same students may be in the unit for three years, content is cycled each three years. A unit team that emphasized facts in social studies might follow a three-year cycle such as United States, one

---

*A more complete description of the sequence is included in the filmstrip *Teaching Units and Lesson Plans* (Los Angeles: VIMCET Associates, 1969).

year; Eastern Hemisphere, one year; Western Hemisphere, one year. A student could start any year in the cycle, since all content units would have a range of objectives. A combined literature/social studies cycle might be "Families," "Communities," and "Countries." A science cycle might be physical science, life science, and earth science. An interdisciplinary cycle on self-concept might be "Uniquely You," "You and Others," and "You and Your World."

A unit team that emphasized concepts might list the concepts and teach them each year. A list of science concepts, for example, might include observing, classifying, communicating, predicting, inferring, measuring, and so on. The student would study these concepts each year he was in the unit, but in a variety of ways and with a variety of materials. For example, during the three-year period the student might classify such items as rocks, simple machines, animals, plants, and library books to master the concept of classifying.*

Grouping in a Content Unit

Grouping in a content unit can be based on pretest data on the facts and concepts emphasized in the unit, or it can be based on student interests.

In a content unit in which facts and concepts are emphasized, each student must accomplish a minimum number of the behavioral objectives. A student is pretested on the required objectives, and then his instructional activities are prescribed, using the pretest results and the student's interest. The student may choose to learn the depth-study objectives or to initiate quest objectives that relate to the unit.

In content units that emphasize concepts or methodologies, grouping can be based on students' interests. For example, in an astronomy unit that emphasized the goals "The student will demonstrate a scientific attitude by formulating conclusions on the basis of evidence" and "The student will use the scientific approach in problem solving," the students were grouped by using focusing questions. At a large group meeting, the teachers explained the content unit. The students were permitted to choose groups such as "Are flying saucers for real?" "What makes stars twinkle?" "Now that

*A more detailed description of this program appears in the filmstrip series *Managing the IGE Learning Program* (Dayton, Ohio: Institute for Development of Educational Activities, 1971).

we're on the moon, where do we go from here?" It did not make any difference which group the student selected. The study focus was on methodologies, not facts.*

Individualized Instructional Packages

One way to individualize is to use a collection of instructional packages and permit student self-selection. UNIPACS and Learning Activity Packages (LAPS) are examples of curriculum packages that can be used in a self-selection program.

A UNIPAC is a self-contained set of teaching-learning materials designed to teach a single idea, skill, or concept. It is structured for individual and independent use in a continuous progress school program.[7]

The UNIPAC format is as follows:

1. *Pretest*—designed to determine readiness, prerequisites, and student need for the lesson.

2. *Main concept*—stated in a declarative sentence.

3. *Component parts*—stated in words or phrases to limit and clarify the declarative sentence.

4. *Behavioral objectives*—the objectives relates directly to the desired terminal performance for each component part.

5. *Instructions for the selection of activities.*

6. *Diversified activities*—three or more activities are available for each objective, to allow student self-selection and/or recycling.

7. *Self-test*—provides feedback for the student; a protection against public failure.

8. *Post-test*—each objective is tested.

9. *Quest*—an opportunity for the student to go beyond the objectives learned.[8]

A Learning Activity Package (LAP) is a form of communication between the student and the teacher that contains instructions for student activities leading toward specified behavior outcomes.[9] A LAP tends to be longer and include more ideas than a UNIPAC.

The LAP format is as follows:

1. *Title*—the primary idea and the secondary ideas of the package are included in this section.

---

*A more detailed description of this program is available in the two IGE 16 mm training films *The Unit Meeting* and *One at a Time, Together* (Dayton, Ohio: Institute for Development of Educational Activities, 1970).

2. *Rationale*—this narrative statement communicates to the student the overall objective of the package and its importance to the student's course of study.

3. *Prerequisite Knowledge Self-Assessment Instrument*—indicates to the student and teacher if the learner possesses the prerequisite knowledge or skills for probable success with the LAP.

4. *Objectives*—designed to guide or structure the behavior of the learner.

5. *Self-evaluation*—this pretest is used to allow the student to by-pass the LAP or to guide the student to those portions of the LAP that he needs to study.

6. *Special Student Directions.*

7. *Learning Activities*—the student is provided a choice of alternatives. A LAP contains a wide range of alternatives in terms of the following: multimedia, multimode, multicontent (different levels of sophistication), and multi-activities.

8. *Post-test*—terminal teacher evaluation is built into the package. [10]

UNIPACS and LAPS are designed to help a student achieve at a pace and level and in a manner commensurate with his unique combination of abilities, previous achievement, cultural background, interests, learning style, and needs. [11] Unit teams or schools should develop or obtain a wide selection of individualized packages so that a self-selection curriculum is available to students.

Interest Grouping

Interest grouping is a plan that provides alternatives for students. Interest grouping can be scheduled for a specific part of the day, cutting across all content discipline lines, or it can be a part of a content unit.

One primary school in Minneapolis uses interest grouping this way. In the morning, students work on skills subjects, such as reading, phonics, and mathematics. In the afternoon, there are two forty-minute periods for which students may select two mini-courses. The mini-courses last three weeks and include a wide range of interests, such as science experiments, creative writing, tumbling, painting, little theater, and great books for children. All the staff and community volunteers teach the mini-courses. Sometimes a course will fill both time blocks. Students sign up for first, second, and third choices. The groups are all multi-age.

One school in Ohio had "Funny Friday" each week. Friday afternoon, the regular school program was replaced with over thirty interest groups, which lasted two hours and met four times. Each month a new list of interest groups was published, and students selected their first and second choices. Groups included academic (foreign languages, science, history), sports (volleyball, modern dance, trampoline), vocational (cooking, woodworking), art, music, etc. One choice was not to go at all. The students who made this choice went to the learning center to study or read.

Interest grouping can also be used within a unit. In one team teaching school, upper elementary students had specific objectives to achieve in a unit on the American Revolution. Three rooms were organized. One room was filled with audio-visual materials for students who wanted to achieve their objectives by viewing or listening. Another room had reading materials—textbooks, workbooks, and trade books. The third room had a teacher who would discuss the American Revolution with the students. A student could choose where and how he would achieve his objectives.

Interest grouping is an excellent way to provide learning options for students. It is a technique that "turns kids on." It turns teachers on, too.

The Learning Station

One of the most exciting ideas for individualized instruction is the learning station.* A learning station is a display, an instructional package, a collection of learning activities, a creative way of teaching. A learning station provides an invitation to the student to learn, to explore, and to discover. It is designed to encourage self-selection, self-direction, and self-motivation.

What makes a learning station? First, a learning station occupies a specific space. This may be a table that has been placed in front of a bulletin board or a screen, desks that have been pushed together, a study carrel, or a mobile hanging from the ceiling. The point is that a learning station is not a variety of materials scattered throughout the classroom. Instead, the necessary components are collected and displayed in an attractive and inviting way in one specific place.

*For a pictorial description of a learning station, *see* the filmstrip set *Managing the IGE Learning Program* (Dayton, Ohio: Institute for Development of Educational Activities, 1971).

Second, a learning station teaches specific objectives. The teacher has specific objectives in mind when she sets up the learning station. Furthermore, the objectives must be clearly stated in language that the students will understand. The main objective of the learning station is physically communicated by title or picture, not necessarily in behavioral terms. It may be a statement: "You can learn to multiply." It may be a question: "How many ways can you multiply?" It may be an invitation: "Let's multiply!"

Third, a learning station provides a variety of learning activities using many different kinds of materials. The activities provide the student with choices of ways to accomplish the objectives in depth. The student can choose from games, practice sheets, audio-visual materials and so on. The range of activities should be appropriate for the students in the unit. The learning station should also include directions that will draw students into pairs or small group study teams. Both the objectives and the activities are arranged in sequence, so that the student can pursue them at his own rate and can achieve appropriate levels of understanding and skills. For example, in the multiplication learning station the sequence might range from beginning multiplication facts to complex multiplication problems. The student selects the activities that are appropriate to him; the range of objectives and activities is wide enough to enable any student in the unit to use the multiplication learning station.

Fourth, a learning station has a built-in management and evaluation system. This system should be designed to encourage student self-direction. Some learning stations direct the students to turn in completed activity sheets. Others have contracts:

I agree to multiply by 2's, 3's, 4's, and 5's.

Signed, *Charles Belinda Rachel*

Others have sign-out sheets for a student to sign when he has satisfactorily met the objective:

I can multiply by 2's, 3's, 4's, and 5's.

Signed, *Charles Belinda Rachel*

Others use appointment sheets, on which the student arranges an evaluation conference (performance test) with the teacher. A learning station must be organized so that the student is directed to the next step or objective.

"We like the idea of learning stations," said the unit leader, "but aren't they time-consuming to make?" Yes, but they are worth it. Learning stations can be used in either skill or content units. They can be used to teach the same concept in different ways. Most teams change their learning stations every three weeks, storing the station for reuse later.

Many cooperating individualized schools (*see* Chapter 11) have a loan system for learning stations. A school staff can develop an amazingly large collection of learning stations in a short time.

The Interest Center

An interest center is a collection of materials for student quest activities. For the student, it is an invitation to learning. The interest center encourages and permits the student to try new activities. It provides an opportunity for students to become self-directive.

An interest center can be a collection of art materials placed on a table. It can be a manipulative bulletin board about magnets. It can be a science table with apparatus and directions for experiments. It can be a projection house equipped with a 16 mm projector with earphones. It can be a quiet reading corner with displays of books and periodicals. It can be a listening station. It can be a research area. It can be a play area.

In an individualized school, corners, halls, windows, and so on can be converted into attractive interest centers. Unlike a learning station, the interest center does not have a specific set of objectives or a management system. It does have a purpose—to build, to test, to read, to view, to listen, to explore.

"It's a fun place. I could stay all day in the science corner. There's microscopes, chemicals, experiments . . ."

"I like Snoopy's Film House best."

The Fully Functioning Media Center

To provide the diversified materials needed in individualized instruction, each school must have a fully functioning media center. Whether it is called the learning center, the library, or the Instructional Materials Center is not important. Individualized instruction requires a library-centered school.

The mission of the media center is to be a working collection of print and nonprint materials, equipment, and personnel so selected, arranged, and located as to serve the needs of the students and teachers and to achieve the goals of the school.

To achieve this mission, the media center must (1) offer a wide range of materials to serve all needs; (2) use various patterns of flexible scheduling so that students can use the materials when they need them; (3) aid teachers in building diversified and effective materials into their instructional programs; and (4) help students develop the skills to fully utilize the resources.[12]

The media center can make readily accessible an extensive variety of materials of varying difficulty and styles. It can become a storehouse of directed and extended materials, enabling the student and the teacher to select and try various learning techniques. Such a collection will include: trade books, textbooks, filmstrips, single concept loop films, 16 mm films, video tapes, pamphlets, pictures, newspapers, magazines, transparencies, records, tapes, cassettes, programed instruction, self-instructional curriculum packages, manipulative devices, models, maps, globes, equipment, and so on.

"Impossible! Our school could never have such a media center!" the teacher from the small school exclaimed. Many teachers have reacted the same way. Yet, it is amazing how many schools have developed functioning media centers. One rural Minnesota school initiated an IGE program. During the first year of implementation, the elementary students shared the high school library, but their use of the library was restricted by the high school students' schedules and use. The individualized instruction program was drastically hampered because there was no elementary media center. The Instructional Improvement Committee (IIC) went to the Board of Education and requested funds for remodeling to build an elementary media center. "No," replied the board chairman, "It's impossible at this time." One of the IIC members, a unit leader, requested and got permission for the school to go to the parents and the community. A signed petition plus a large turnout of the community at the next board meeting changed the decision. This year the school has a remodeled, carpeted media center staffed by a professional librarian.

To start a media center, the school staff should first centralize all instructional materials. The closets and cabinets of all classrooms should be emptied and the materials organized in a central place. Second, the materials should be cataloged so that they can be used easily by students and teachers. Third, students and teachers should be taught to use the materials and equipment. Fourth, a flexible plan for the use of the media center by both students and teachers should be developed. Fifth, a budget should be developed for the media center so that the IIC and the librarian can select and order those materials necessary to achieve an individualized program.

The kind of media center described above requires a new kind of librarian, unlike the one who kept books stacked in neat rows and piles, and, in answer to the question "How's it going?" replied, "Fine. There are two books out, but I think I can get them back this afternoon."

The school librarian must know diversified learning materials. He must like students. He must be able to teach students the necessary skills to use the materials efficiently. He must make the media center an exciting, meaningful place where students love to come. The school librarian must be able to work with teachers and the IIC. He must help them develop curriculum programs with diversified materials. He must participate in curriculum revision and implementation. He must facilitate the teachers' use of media.

A fully functioning media center staffed by an excellent librarian may be a difficult goal, but it is a goal worth striving for. The media center plays a key role in an individualized school program.

*Students must be taught to work efficiently
in an individualized program.*

Chapter 8
Managing an
Individualized
Program

"But where are the other kids?" the teacher from a traditional school asked. "In all the films about individualized instruction, or when you talk about how you teach in your unit, we see teachers working in small groups or with one student. Where are the other kids when she's doing this?"

"You mean how does the unit team manage the program so that a teacher can teach in the one-to-one or small group mode and at the same time have appropriate learning activities for the other students?" responded the unit leader.

"I guess that's what I mean," answered the teacher. "Where are the other kids?"

Managing is a stumbling block for many teachers attempting to implement individualized instruction. How do we schedule? What kinds of records should we keep? What kinds of rules should we make? How can we keep students from getting lost? These are questions to which concerned teachers are seeking answers. An examination of some of the successful strategies good teachers and effective unit teams have used can serve as a guide for a teacher or team planning to individualize.

Developing a Unit Identity

Changing a school from a graded, self-contained classroom organization into individualized, nongraded, multi-age, team-taught units is a major change for teachers and students. Managing such a program is an example of the unit team's philosophy of education put into practice.

Management in effective individualized programs is based on the principle that both students and teachers are trustworthy. The old question "How can a student become trustworthy unless someone trusts him?" is appropriate. Unit teachers trust students. They believe that students want to learn and will learn if given the opportunity. Unit teachers trust each other. They believe that each unit teacher will do her share to make the individualized program effective. Unit teams trust the other teachers in the school. Through the Instructional Improvement Committee (IIC), the teachers share the responsibility for the education of the boys and girls in the school. Management based on trust is the self-fulfilling prophecy in action.*

A unit is a new organizational structure. It replaces the grade or the classroom. In a traditional school, being able to say, "I'm in grade 5," or, "I'm in Mrs. Noffsinger's room," gave a student an identity. Each unit in an individualized school should strive to build a special identity of its own. Every student should understand and be able to explain to his family and friends where the unit is, what it stands for, and what it does.

A unit should occupy a specific geographic space or area within the school building. The location, such as Classrooms 111, 112, and 113 or the Blue Pod, gives a unit a spatial identity.

A student should know what a unit stands for. The unit team should emphasize and explain the unit's goals (the desired student outcomes and the philosophy of the unit team). When students understand the goals of the unit, an *esprit de corps* or a sense of pride begins to develop.

Large group meetings can be used to develop a unit identity. These meetings can be morning exercises, such as a song or pledge, or they can be a preview of what will happen that day. Some units select names—such as the Beavers, the Big Dipper Unit, the Zoo Unit, and the Coppy Cats—and mascots. Some units select songs to open the school day, some choose unit colors, and some even order unit sweatshirts. All efforts should be made to give the unit an identity that will help the students achieve the goals of the unit and will enhance each student's self-concept.

---

*Unit teams that assume that students cannot be trusted and that they must be supervised closely can individualize instruction, but it will take a much higher adult-student ratio than the unit team that trusts students.

The following comments are from students in units that have developed identities.

"It's great to be in the Beaver Unit. We're the hardest working and hardest playing group you've ever seen."

"How'd you like to be in the Zoo Unit? A kid can be different. We don't have to all be the same. We can learn things in our own way."

"Big Dipper! Big Dipper! We're the 'star' unit! Big Dipper! Big Dipper! We're the 'star' unit!"

If the school has a student council (and it should), students can be elected to represent the unit at student council meetings. Then student problems that cross unit lines can be presented to the student council or the IIC, whichever group seems to be appropriate.

In building a unit identity, the unit team should remember the following management strategies:

1. *Emphasize the goals of the unit.* Students should be focused to achieve these goals.

2. *Place the emphasis on learning, not teaching.*

3. *Keep the schedule simple and flexible.*

4. *Don't try to have each student at a different place.* Do use small groups and student teams. Build skill groups that use unit team members, resource teachers, and instructional aides to provide students with options. Put students for whom the options are not appropriate in independent study or in helping roles.

5. *Train students to work efficiently in an individualized program.* Students should be able to explain the diagnostic-prescriptive learning cycle (objective, pre-assessment, diversified learning activities, post-assessment). Each student should be able to state the objectives that he is currently working to achieve.

6. *Train older students to help younger students.* The helping relationship should be emphasized. Instead of being resentful of younger students, older students should be taught to assume roles as tutors and models. They can assume some of the responsibility for helping younger students learn and adjust.

7. *Don't keep problems to yourself.* If the unit team thinks that a student is too noisy or not doing appropriate work, the teachers should share the problem with the student or with his parents.

Scheduling

The schedule should not be so complex that the unit team spends the majority of its meeting time scheduling. A simple schedule with large, interchangeable blocks of time is the easiest plan to manage.

Dividing the school day into three or four large blocks of time has proven to be manageable. The block schedule provides flexibility for the unit team and permits more efficient use of instructional aides and specialists. The daily schedule shown below is an example of how large blocks of time can be used.

Time	Block
8:30–10:00	Block A
10:00–11:30	Block B
11:30–12:15	Lunch
12:15– 1:45	Block C
1:45– 3:15	Block D

One unit team used the block schedule in the following way. Block A was used for skill development groups in reading and for language arts/social studies activities. Block B was used for skill development groups in mathematics and study skills. During Blocks A and B, instructional aides, supplemental teachers, and special-education teachers were scheduled into the unit to provide more options. Block C was used for special subjects, such as physical education, art, and music. Specialists in these areas were scheduled into the unit during Block C. (In schools where such specialists are not available, unit teachers, with parent volunteers and older students, can teach the special subjects. Block D was used for the content unit, which might be science, social studies, health, litera-ture, or an interdisciplinary combination of subjects.

A flexible schedule such as this enables the IIC to schedule special teachers and instructional aides efficiently. It also enables the unit team to change what occurs in each block readily, so that scheduling does not demand a high percentage of the unit team's planning time.

Managing Skill Groups

Once every student in the unit has been pretested and is studying an appropriate behavioral objective, a unit team needs a method for managing the skill development program.

First, *there must be an appropriate record-keeping system.* If the unit team plans to place students in skill development small groups, pretest results must be organized into a usable system. Some schools make charts for display in the unit team's planning room. These charts include the continuum of behavioral objectives. They have pockets or slots in which to place the names of the students studying a specific objective. The name of the teacher who is instructing this objective is also included on the chart, so that by glancing at the chart one can see what objectives every student in the unit is studying and which teacher is teaching him. When a student masters an objective, this is recorded in his cumulative file and his card is moved to another slot on the chart.

Some skill programs, such as the Wisconsin Reading Design, use specially punched cards to record student data. The pretest data are recorded on each student's card with the objectives that he has mastered notched open. When the unit team wants to identify the students who need work on a specific objective, a skewer is run through the cards and the records of the students who need to study the objective are lifted out. When a student masters the objective, his card is notched. Keeping records in this way allows a unit team to identify student needs and to build instructional groups from assessment data.

Second, *there must be a plan for teaching a number of skills at the same time.* One efficient way is to teach all the word attack skill groups at the same time. To provide more options, remedial teachers, supplemental teachers, and instructional aides can be assigned to the unit. In this way, unit teachers can instruct more than one skill group.

At one school, four unit teachers were scheduled in the following way during Individualized Mathematics Study (IMS). One had all the students who were working on addition and subtraction prescriptions in one room. Another teacher in another room had multiplication and division. A third had fractional numbers. The fourth had measurement. Students went to the room where their prescriptions directed them. The advantages of this system were (1) teacher preparation was easier, (2) multi-age grouping was accomplished, and (3) all the teachers saw all the students in mathematics.

Unit teams usually schedule a specific time for a skill development group to master the skill. Many use a two-week period. At the end of this time, all students are given the post-test. If a student has not mastered the skill, he should be recycled to study the same skill at a later date.*

In a skill program such as IMS or Individually Prescribed Instruction (IPI), each student works independently on his own prescription. To efficiently manage such a program, instructional aides, parent volunteers, or student aides are scheduled to work with the classroom teachers as the students are working on their prescriptions. The aides check tests and work sheets, provide materials for students, and give students help. There is a danger in this program that too much help can build a dependency relationship rather than enable students to become independent, self-directed students. Some unit teams build student study teams if they find students becoming too dependent on teachers or aides. Other teams instruct a student to ask another student first if he does not understand the directions. There are, of course, a lot more questions raised during skill groups such as this. The same questions are probably there when teachers lecture, but the student doesn't have a chance to ask them.

Third, *there must be a feedback system so that a student understands his diagnosis, prescription, and progress.* Each student should be able to state the learning objective that he is trying to achieve. He should also be able to explain his skill profile (chart, notched card, etc.) to others.

Fourth, *skill-group teaching must not be all independent study.* Independent activities can be over-emphasized in skill group teaching. Some students may work so slowly that they never develop the necessary speed in mathematics computations. Other students may hurry through their work because they think that passing the post-test is the only thing that is important. Time must be set aside during the skill development groups for drill, either at the chalkboard or at desks. Time must also be provided for activities that motivate the student to master new skills. In the skill development group, the teacher does not teach in the traditional manner very often. But when she does, every effort should be made to make the teaching exciting, fun, and meaningful.

PEP—A Kindergarten Skill Development Program

The kindergartens in Montevideo, Minnesota, are an example of a

---

*The reader may want to review the section "The Skill Development Small Group" on pp. 59-60.

skill group program in action. These kindergartens use the Primary Education Project (PEP), an individualized instructional program designed for kindergarten students who have not yet developed reading skills. The program was developed by the University of Pittsburgh to prepare younger students for IPI. This program pretests, prescribes instruction, and post-tests students in six areas: Quantification, General Motor, Classification, Auditory, Visual Motor, and Numerals and Letters.

The Montevideo kindergarten classrooms are divided into three general areas: the testing area, the work area, and the exploratory area. As the PEP period begins, each student finds his prescribed lesson for the day on a card placed in his library card pocket on the bulletin board. The student's prescription directs him to specific labeled boxes. PEP is a "shoe box curriculum." The readiness activities that have traditionally been taught in kindergarten are organized for individualized instruction. Each objective is translated into student activities, which are placed in a box. Students count, match, compare, make patterns, and so on. As the students work, the classroom teacher or instructional aides travel among the students to guide and to check the work being done. Since physical readiness objectives are included in PEP, each child is in a small group for physical education each day. During work time, some students are tested by the teacher or an aide, who gives a performance test and charts the student's progress. When a student's work for the day is completed and checked, he returns his boxes to the proper places and moves to the exploratory area. In this free-play area, students may select from a number of unstructured activities.

Teachers at Montevideo have found that the instructional range of the class members increases greatly as the year progresses. They have found that kindergarten students can learn more skills more quickly in an individualized program. Many of the Montevideo students begin reading much earlier. PEP is motivating; students are eager to "do their boxes" each day. The challenge to the classroom teacher is to keep a good balance of prescribed, structured instruction and unstructured instruction. The active, curious five-year-old needs time to inquire, share, construct, dramatize, verbalize, and solve problems of many kinds.

Managing Content Units

One block of time in the daily schedule should be used for content units or for interest grouping.*

The "umbrella" content unit, in which all students study the same subject (but have different objectives), is both a high-interest and an efficient way to manage content subjects. Such a unit can emphasize the concepts of one discipline, or it can be inter-disciplinary. For example, a unit entitled "Magnet Magic" emphasizes science concepts only, while a unit entitled "Pollution Problems" combines science and social studies.

It is good management not to schedule two umbrella content units or two high-interest units at the same time. One team, for example, taught no social studies while a three-week unit in science was being taught. This plan helps keep the daily schedule workable.

In the umbrella content unit, the unit is introduced in a large group meeting, where student responsibilities and options are described. Clear-cut assignments are given, so that each student knows what he is required to do and what his options can be. Small groups may then spin out of the large group to provide an opportunity for individual prescriptions to be explained and for students to discuss options with a teacher.

If the content unit focuses around learning stations, each learning station can be introduced at large group sessions. If the content unit provides different study options, such as a reading room, an audio-visual room, a small group discussion room, or a project room, an explanation of how the student can use these spaces is included in the large group meeting.

Since a content unit lasts two or three weeks, directions must be reviewed or new instructions must be given to the students every two or three days. The key thing that a unit team must remember is not to keep problems to themselves, but to share them with the students. The unit team is responsible for training the students to function in an individualized program. The content unit is a good place to train students to become more responsible, self-directed learners.

Small groups are an important mode in the content unit. Managing time so that teachers can work with small groups is sometimes a problem. To free some teachers to work with brain-

---

*Interest grouping can also be used for managing short content courses. The reader may want to review the section "Interest Grouping" on pp. 79-80.

storming, study, inquiry, discursive, or Socratic small groups, other unit teachers may supervise larger numbers of students who are working independently or in study teams. One teacher can efficiently direct a number of task or workshop small groups at the same time.

Record keeping in content units will vary from school to school. The record-keeping policy must be developed by the IIC, so that there is communication between units. Since a student is in a unit for two or three years, records must be kept of content units presented. Records of objectives or concepts mastered and projects or quest activities completed are usually kept also. These records must be forwarded to the next unit, so that they can be built upon and expanded.

Management Forms

A number of sample forms for managing individualized programs have been developed. These forms vary; some are very complex, and some are very simple. Unit teams may want to use the following sample forms as models for developing their own management forms.

Contracts

An efficient way of both goal-setting and managing an individualized learning program is the contract. During a goal-setting conference, the student and teacher set appropriate goals to be achieved during the coming week. The use of a contract provides a management system for this program.

Contracts can be very simple. For example:

This week I agree to work the following units:

1. _____
2. _____
3. _____

Signed _____

Date _____

Teacher's Signature _____

```
┌─────────────────────────────────────────────────────────┐
│                    Student Contract                      │
│   Name_____      Date _____       │
│   Student Objectives                                     │
│                                                          │
│   Student Signature _____         │
│   Completion Date _____         │
│   Teacher's Signature _____         │
└─────────────────────────────────────────────────────────┘
```

Students working in areas where no prepared materials are available may use a contract form such as the following.

```
┌─────────────────────────────────────────────────────────┐
│                    Quest Contract                        │
│   Content _____          │
│   Purpose _____          │
│   Performance Objective(s) _____          │
│   _____           │
│   Evaluation Plan _____          │
│   _____           │
│   Suggested Materials and Activities _____          │
│   _____           │
│   Resources _____          │
│                                                          │
│   I, _____, agree to complete by_____ │
│   Any change in the plan must be agreed upon by my teacher│
│   and me.                                                │
│   Teacher's Signature_____          │
└─────────────────────────────────────────────────────────┘
```

Reading Conferences

The idea of learning to read by reading is the heart of an individualized reading program. Following is the introduction to a booklet used in an IGE school in Oregon, Wisconsin. A few of the forms in the booklet are also shown.

Dear Student,

This booklet has been prepared for you to give you a clear idea of what our individualized reading program expects of you.

Since each of you is different, different things are expected from each student. Some of you will read animal stories, some mysteries, some fantasy, and some, still other types of books. The *one* thing you all have in common is the need to read. Some will read several books in a week, others may read less, perhaps not even a complete book in one week. This is your individualized reading. The only thing that is expected of you is that the reading you do is appropriate to your reading level, that you are reading, and that you are enjoying it. You will also use any of the media in the Learning Center that you wish to for enrichment.

We will have individual conferences at *least* once a week. During these conferences you will tell me about the reading work you are doing. You will keep a record of all the work you do in this booklet. We will evaluate your reading. This means we will check on your reading skills and try to improve on the ones you are weak in.

Most important of all, I want you to learn how much pleasure you can get from books; how much more exciting and full your life can become through books. There are many places we can never visit, but we can go *anywhere* in a book.

See you there.

My Own Reading Objectives

Name _____

_____

_____

_____

_____

How to Prepare for a Conference

1. Read a selection.
2. List any new word you find.
3. Be prepared to tell why you chose your book.
4. Bring a selection or another book you will be reading next.
5. Make a selection you will read orally to your teacher.
6. Summarize briefly what you have read.
7. Be prepared to briefly discuss the main characters and events.
8. Bring along your list of books read.
9. Bring along your reading booklet.

My Enrichment Reading Chart

Book Title, Article Story, etc.	Date	Pages Read	Comments

Reaching for Distances in Meanings Every Day!

New words extend the enjoyment of reading. When you find an unfamiliar word, use your dictionary. If you find several meanings for the same word, the sentence in which it is used will help you choose the exact idea the author wanted to give.

Date	New Word	Phrase or sentence in the story	Dictionary Meaning
Sept. 9	malady	Rain and cold were responsible for the *malady*.	sickness, disease

Independent Activities

The following are samples of forms that can be used for managing independent study activities.

Science Television Program Report

Name _____

Date _____

Complete the following information on the program you watched:

Name of the Program _____

Channel ____ Date _____ Time _____

1. Give a short summary of the program (approximately 50 words)

2. What did you like the most about the program? What interested you the most?

3. What did you not like about the program? Any criticisms?

4. What did the program have to say about how MAN is harming the environment?

5. What did the program have to say about how MAN is helping the environment?

6. Would you watch another program on a similar topic?

7. Would you watch another program on a different topic, but put on by the same company?

Book Report

Name _____

Date _____

Complete the following information from the book you read:

Title _____

Author _____

Publisher _____

Date of Publication _____

1. If you liked the book, tell why (what interested you the most).

2. If there was anything you did not like about the book, tell what it was.

3. If there were illustrations or pictures, how did they make things more clear?

4. What level reader would find this book the most interesting? (good, average, poor)

5. Why would you recommend the book to a friend?

6. Would you read another book on a similar topic?

Independent Directed Study

Name _____

Teacher _____

Date _____

I plan to do independent study in
Problem or question I plan to study:

Plan for study (be as specific as you can at this time):

What I hope to learn or how I plan to change as a result of this study:

How I plan to evaluate my achievement and communicate what I have learned to my teacher, parents, and to other students:

Directions and Study Schedules

It is often hard for a student to manage his time efficiently while working on UNIPACS or LAPS. One school uses the following directions and study schedule to help students manage their time in such a program.

Guidelines for Laps

1. Read directions carefully.
2. Ask your instructor and friends for help when needed.
3. Record data, answers, and notes neatly and accurately.
4. Handle all equipment carefully and return all equipment in good condition (clean, complete, on time).
5. Use self-tests *after* you have studied.
6. Have all work in order for approval by instructor when you arrive at an evaluation checkpoint.
7. Plan ahead and use time wisely.

Study Schedule

Mark in the date on which you begin the LAP. Enter the date that the packet is to be completed. Plan your schedule to make the best use of the time available.

SUN	MON	TUE	WED	THURS	FRI	SAT

Guiding Students

Since homerooms are eliminated in an individualized program, there is a danger that a unit team may lose track of a student or that a student may feel that individualized instruction is lonely and depersonalized. Each unit team must develop a plan for checking student progress and guiding each student.

Teams must schedule regular meetings to check on the progress of each individual student in the unit. Is the contract appropriate? Is the student mastering skills at an acceptable rate? Is the quality of his work satisfactory? Have his prescriptions been appropriate? What are the student's best learning styles? After a student's progress has been reviewed, a teacher should give the student feedback. "Joe, the team reviewed your progress last night. You're doing fine!" Or "Joe, the team reviewed your progress last night. You need more time for math objectives. Let's build your contract next week so that you have more time scheduled in the math area."

Each student should have the special attention of one teacher. This is not a retreat to the self-contained classroom. The teacher is responsible for the guidance functions of a specific group of students.

The teacher and the student meet once each week. This one-to-one session is used to check the student's progress and to set goals for the next week. The student shares what he is doing and why, how he is feeling, and what problems he has. The teacher gives the student feedback, checks his progress, and helps the student finalize a contract for the coming week.

The teacher is accountable. She has the overall responsibility for planning and tracking the learning achievement of the student. She shares this responsibility with the student, helping the student to become self-directive and self-motivating. The teacher provides opportunities so that the student can assume increasing responsibility for the selection of his own learning objectives.

Most important, because one teacher is responsible for the guidance function the student feels that there is someone who is especially concerned for him, someone that he can come to for help at any time.

This teacher is also responsible for reporting to the student's parents. She holds parent conferences and follows up on absenteeism or other signs of problems.

To manage these guidance functions, some unit teachers organize small, multi-age core groups. This grouping pattern permits open discussion of student problems. It provides a supportive peer group that can help a student learn, grow, and develop his individuality.

*In individualizing instruction, don't start by
drastically changing the reporting system.
Change reporting procedures at the same
pace that the instructional program is
changed.*

Chapter 9
Communicating
with Parents

"Since our program is now individualized, should we report to parents?" asked a unit teacher.

"Absolutely," answered the unit leader. "Individualizing does not mean doing away with reporting. The school has an obligation to report to both the student and the parent. It's the whole concept of feedback. The child has a right to know how he's doing; so do his parents."

"But our old report card just doesn't fit the concept of criterion-referenced teaching. How do we report the objectives a student has mastered in the slots on an A-B-C grade card? We'll have to design a new system."

This dialogue occurs in almost every school before or soon after the individualized program begins. Planning a program for parent communication is an important task. School staffs often want to change the reporting system first, but this is a simple solution to the complex problem of communication. *A school should not start by drastically changing the reporting system.* Sometimes it is easier to change the school from a traditional program to an individualized one than it is to change the grading program.

In one individualized school, the school staff carefully designed a parent conference in which the teacher reported the student's pretest scores, the objectives that he had mastered, and the objectives that he was working on. A formal observation chart describing the student's learning style and his peer relations was also explained to the parent. To test this new form, two sets of parents volunteered to have their conferences before the entire faculty. After the parents had had a chance to ask the teacher questions, they said, "You know, that's the most and best kind of information we've ever had about our child. You're going to send us a report card, too, aren't you?"

It is harder for parents to accept change in reporting than in probably any other area. As one parent said, "Maybe A-B-C-D report cards don't say anything to you educators. But I surely know how to feel about my child when the card is all A's and B's or when it's C's and D's."

In individualizing instruction, a school staff should consider both the total school communication program and specific methods of reporting student progress.

The Basis for Communication

Schools exist for children. All that is done to establish and maintain the school program must be measured in terms of what is best for each child. The purpose of the communication program in an individualized school is to improve the quality and appropriateness of the educational program. Good communication is essential.

There is much evidence that the public has lost faith in the schools over the past few years. Broken promises by school administrators, teacher negotiations, and frequent tax-increasing money issues have caused the public to question school practices. In individualizing instruction, a school staff must work to regain the trust of the parents and the community. To do this, the staff must develop an effective school communication program.

The premise for a staff individualizing instruction to remember is that parents love their children. Parents do want the best educational program possible for their children. If a school staff can *communicate* and *demonstrate* that individualized instruction puts children first, faith and trust in the schools can be developed.

There is nothing more important than developing a trusting relationship among students, parents, teachers, and community members. Trust can be built on a two-way communication system; the school must develop a process both to send information to the community and to listen for community feedback. Trust can be built if the communication system is on-going; communicating only when a school issue is to be passed or a new program is being implemented can be negative and will not develop a trusting relationship. Trust can be built if the communication is direct; frequent parent-teacher contact can build a trusting relationship. Trust can be built if communication is personal; parents want feedback about their children and the opportunity to talk about their children's academic and social growth.

Communication is never more vital than at the time when a school is implementing an innovative program. Because a good communication program can build a trusting relationship, everyone—the students, the parents, the staff, and the community—benefits from good communication.

The Communication Program in the Individualized School

Communication about individualized instruction is a three-step process. Step One is before the individualizing program begins. Step Two is the initial implementation (the first few months of individualization). Step Three is the on-going communication program. While the principal is the chief communicator in all three steps, all staff should have a role in the school communication program.*

Communication about the individualized instruction program begins before the new program is implemented. Letters reflecting the intent to individualize are sent to parents. An assembly is held to explain the new program to the students who will be in it the following year. The principal explains the new program to the school secretaries, custodians, cooks, and bus drivers. News articles are released to local and school newspapers. Parent meetings are held to explain the new school organization and some of the components of individualized instruction. Newsletters that describe teaching by objectives, multi-unit organization, teaming, and so on are sent to parents and interested community members. The classroom teachers explain the placement for the next school year directly to each student. A letter explaining this placement is sent to the parents.

During the initial implementation of the individualized instruction program, good communication is crucial. A letter reviewing the new program is sent to each student. News articles about the program are released to the local newspapers. Materials about the new

---

*Individually Guided Education: Principal's Handbook, by Joan Beugen, Ira Kerns, and Norman Graper (Dayton, Ohio: Institute for Development of Educational Activities, 1971), pp. 45-67, gives a more complete description of this public relations program.

program are prepared, distributed, and explained to students the first day of school. A unit open house should be held during the first month of school to give parents a chance to meet the unit teachers and to learn the unit plans for the year. Individualized instruction is explained, and time is provided for parents' questions. At this meeting, parents are elected as unit representatives on the Parent Advisory Council.

The on-going program is designed to develop a trust relationship between the unit team and the parents. Primarily, the unit team does this by sending home a happy, educated student each day. The communication program includes (1) regularly scheduled unit parent meetings, (2) a Parent Advisory Council, (3) parent-teacher conferences, (4) parent volunteers, and (5) newsletters and newspaper articles.

The unit parent meetings may replace or supplement the meetings of the parent-teacher organization. At these meetings, teachers present what the unit is doing, display student work, explain components of the individualized program, and suggest ways parents can help their children in learning. The unit parent meetings are designed to provide direct contact between unit teachers and parents. One unit team had a private pact that one of them would talk directly to every parent who came to the meetings. It was amazing to see how this kind of behavior affected both the parents and the teachers. A trusting relationship did develop. For example, one Appalachian father shared, "I was always afraid of school and educated people. These teachers made me and my Bobby both feel important." The unit parent meeting is the ideal place to start developing trust.

The Parent Advisory Council is a school-wide organization made up of representative parents from each unit and the members of the Instructional Improvement Committee (IIC). This group meets monthly, not to set policy but to offer advice. It reacts to issues of concern to the school. It promotes mutual understanding and provides feedback to school personnel. The IIC can consider parent ideas for resolving problems and improving school operation. The Parent Advisory Council can help make the changes and adjustments required for individualized instruction to take place.[1]

One feature of the on-going school communication program is the use of parent volunteers. Individualized instruction requires many hands. There are a number of ways parents can help the school. In one nongraded school, over fifty mothers worked as volunteers in an individualized physical education program, helping students in body management exercises. Another school used parent volunteers in the clinic. Others used them in the learning center, in the office, in the units, in the lunchroom, and on the playground. In interest groups, parents can volunteer as resource persons in special areas, providing more alternatives within the instructional program. The parent volunteer program is a good way to communicate individualized instruction to parents.

In the on-going communication program, the principal should publish regular newsletters. One way to make publishing newsletters regular is to include a calendar of events in each one. This feature encourages families to use the newsletter. The principal should also release news articles regularly.

Reporting student progress and parent-teacher conferences are important aspects of the on-going school communication program.

Reporting Student Progress

Reporting student progress is really an off-shoot of the all-important function of evaluation. A system of student evaluation should do five things. One, it should facilitate self-evaluation. After the report is generated, a student, parent, or teacher should be able to prescribe learning activities. Two, the evaluation system should encompass every objective valued by the school. Often schools report only in the skill areas, which are easier to report. Content and affective objectives should be included in the report as well. Three, it should produce useful student records. If the data reported is not helpful to the unit teachers who are teaching the student, it is questionable if it should be reported. For example, Mrs. Wright used to stay up late at night trying to decide whether or not to give a particular student a B— or a C+. After she finally made her decision, it was discouraging to find that the student's next teacher never looked at grades from previous years. Fourth, the evaluation system should facilitate learning and teaching. In some schools, students are so "uptight" about grades that absenteeism increases greatly on the day report cards are issued. Fifth, it should provide feedback that enables the school staff to answer larger questions about curriculum development and educational policy.[2]

In designing an evaluation system, the school staff should also consider the difference between an individualized program and a traditional one. In an individualized program the goals of the school are translated into behavioral objectives. A student is required to do some objectives; he may choose to do some objectives; or, he may develop some of his own objectives. In such a program there is a need for both criterion-referenced reporting and normative reporting.

Criterion-Referenced Reporting

Criterion-referenced reporting requires that both students and parents understand the concept of teaching by objectives. The Learning Cycle—objective, pre-assessment, diversified learning activities, and post-assessment—must be explained. The reporting will then become a "Yes-No" system. These are the objectives the student has mastered; these are the objectives he is working on now; these are the objectives he will be working on. Schools that use criterion-referenced reporting find the "Yes-No" system much more demanding than A-B-C-D grades. If Colleen's objective is to add unlike fractions with 80 percent accuracy, for example, Colleen will not begin another objective until she masters this one. In the traditional system, the demands were not this high; Colleen would move to the next concept either when her class moved or when she achieved 70 percent, 65 percent, or even 60 percent accuracy. Criterion-referenced reporting in skill subjects is particularly helpful to both the student and parent because the student's progress can be charted clearly and new goals can be set.

On the following pages are some examples of criterion-referenced progress sheets for reading, mathematics, and social studies.

Word Attack Skills Mastered

Name_____

*Date					
Level C 1. Sight Vocabulary					
2. Consonant Variants					
3. Consonant Blends					
4. Long Vowel Sounds					
5. Vowel +r, al, aw					
6. Diphthongs					
7. Long and Short oo					
8. Vowel Rules					
Short vowel					
Silent e rule					
Final vowel					
9. Consonant Digraphs					
10. Prefixes and Suffixes					
11. Plurals					
12. Homonyms					
13. Synonyms and Antonyms					
14. Multiple Word Meanings					

*Put in the date that the skill was started and when mastered.

Mathematics Progress Report

Student _____

Level III

Date_____	Date_____	Date_____
Pretest	Post-test	Retest
Score_____	Score_____	Score_____

Addition facts through 10
Subtraction facts through 10
Mastery of two-figure numerals
Write three-figure numerals 101-150
Count three-figure numerals 101-150
Progressed to Level IV Date_____Teacher_____

Level IV

Date_____	Date_____	Date_____
Pretest	Post-test	Retest
Score_____	Score_____	Score_____

Count and recognize through 200
Addition facts through 12
Subtraction facts through 12
Two- and three-place addition columns (no regrouping)
Two-place subtraction (no regrouping)
Setting up number sentences
Choosing correct process in number stories
Progressed to Level V Date_____Teacher_____

Individual's Course Objectives in Social Studies[3]
(Teacher-student developed according to student's ability)

Objective	Apparent Success	
	High	Low
The Death of a Republic: *A Study from Roman History* 1. To develop an ability to examine original historical source material and make reasoned judgments from it	———————→	
2. To develop an ability to make inferences about social and political processes in general from a particular exemplary historical situation	————————————→	
3. To develop social studies research skills	—→	
4. To acquire information about Roman history and civilization	——————————————→	

*Normative Reporting**

Criterion-referenced reporting gives the student and his parents information about the student's progress in relation to a set of objectives. It does not, however, provide data for two questions that parents want answered: "Is he working up to his potential?" and "How does his work compare with other students his age?" Schools

---

*The author is aware that normative reporting is a controversial subject. This section is included because personnel in individualized schools have found that it is helpful to report normative data in skill areas such as reading, mathematics, and language usage to communicate to the parents that the student is making appropriate progress. One danger is that it opens the teacher for the parents' question, "How's Tommy doing in relation to the other kids in his class?" Answering this question puts the unitized school organization right back into graded, competitive classes. Teachers have the difficult task of teaching parents that this is an inappropriate question.

have an obligation to provide parents with normative data about the individual student. This includes (1) a complete and accurate picture of the student's own potentiality and the extent to which his progress in school measures up to that potential, and (2) an approximate description of the way the student's progress compares with other students his age throughout the United States.[4]

Normative data can be obtained by using standard achievement and intelligence tests. The problem has been how to share this normative data with students and parents. One school found the following system successful. Scores on both the achievement and intelligence tests were converted into stanines and were reported to students and parents in the following way.

"Mrs. Green, you can see we have converted all our scores into a nine-point scale." (The teacher showed the parent the following diagram and *did not* call the scores stanines.) "1, 2, and 3 are low; 4, 5, and 6 are average; and 7, 8, and 9 are high."

1	2	3	4	5	6	7	8	9
LOW			AVERAGE			HIGH		

"By using this scale, we can compare Debbie's capacity to her achievement. We can check to see if she's working up to her potential."

"This looks interesting," said Mrs. Green.

"One more thing before we look at her scores," continued the teacher. "These tests are not 100 percent reliable. At our school, we say that if the test varies one point there really isn't any difference. For example, if a student's verbal I.Q. was 5 and his reading vocabulary score was 4, we'd say that he is working up to his capacity. If it was 3, we might retest him or study his daily work. Now, let's look at Debbie's scores. Any questions before we begin?"

The same teacher might share Debbie's achievement test scores with her in this way. (This works with students as young as seven or eight years old.)

"Debbie, here's a profile of your achievement test scores. We've arranged these scores into a nine-point scale." (She shows Debbie the diagram.) "Now, which of the subtests have you done best in?"

Debbie studies the sheet and answers, "Reading. I've got a 7 in vocabulary and an 8 in comprehension."

"Yes," replied the teacher. "Those are good scores." (Debbie's verbal I.Q. score was 7.) "What area do you need to work in?"

"Spelling. My score is 5. That's my lowest score. I can be a better speller than that."

"Yes, I believe you can," said the teacher. "Who can help you improve your spelling?"

"I think I should work more in Mr. Leigh's spelling group," answered Debbie.

"Okay. Let's put that on your next few contracts."

The Student-Parent-Teacher Conference

The parent conference is the best way to achieve direct and personal communication about student progress in an individualized school. A good conference produces effective and clear communication between the school and the home. It has the potential for providing more information and better understanding. A parent can't ask questions to a report card. Misunderstandings that occur in written reports can be eliminated in a conference. Either the parent or the teacher can raise questions for information or clarification.

The primary purpose of a parent conference is to communicate student progress to parents. For this to happen, each parent must understand the individualized instruction program used in the school. At the first conference, the teacher explains the diagnostic-prescriptive learning cycle. Parents are shown that their child is evaluated on the basis of his individual mastery of learning objectives. The teacher shows, or provides the parents with, a list of the objectives the student has mastered and the ones he is currently studying. The teacher describes the student's learning style and explains how it influences the choice of learning activities for the student. The teacher also explains how individualized instruction helps the student to learn independently and to become self-directive. Some schools use a checklist to report and evaluate student behavior in the affective domain.

Time should be set aside in the conference for the parents to discuss their children, to ask questions and express their concerns about their child's education. Parents should be encouraged to explain their observations about the student to the teacher. Listening to parents can help teachers gain insights that will enable individualized programs to meet the needs of the student.[5]

The student may also participate in the conference. The student-parent-teacher conference is especially appropriate for an individualized program. The student used to be the last person to find out how he was doing in school. In an individualized program, the student should be the first to know. He should know what he is doing well and what he is having problems with. If the student does not attend the conference, the teacher should discuss with him in advance what will be said to the parents.[6]

One school has a very interesting student-parent-teacher conference plan. Before the conference, the teacher reviews all the information with the student. Then the student conducts the conference and presents all materials to the parent. The teacher serves as a resource person to provide information that the student cannot answer. Older elementary students can handle this responsibility quite effectively.

Most schools have found that three or four conferences per year are necessary. Individualized instruction must be explained. Student progress must be reported. Standard test scores must be reported. The student's placement for the next school year should be discussed. Either the parent or the unit teacher should schedule additional conferences as needed. More frequent conferences may be appropriate the year a student changes schools or units.

One parent complaint about conferences has been lack of follow-up. A technique that has worked for many teachers is to set a date for a phone call to follow up on the problem.

Conferences can be individualized, too. One school sends parents a conference pre-planning sheet. The parents list the areas and concerns they want to discuss during the conference. Another school sends home a pre-conference check sheet. Parents check three topics that they definitely want discussed at the conference. Again, this method is especially appropriate for an individualized instruction program.

Most individualized schools use conferences for reporting to parents. Because only one parent attends the conference, many schools prepare copies of the student's progress reports for the parents. This helps the student and the parent who attended the conference to explain what was discussed to the other parent.

Changing Reporting Systems

School staffs in individualized school programs use the following six methods for reporting student progress: (1) they continue to use traditional report cards; (2) they use both report cards and parent-teacher conferences; (3) they use report cards and student-parent-teacher conferences; (4) they use conferences alone; (5) they develop new report forms; (6) they de-emphasize reporting and do not report formally at all.

Individualized instruction is not implemented in all subjects at the same time. During the first year a school usually individualizes in only one skill subject and one content subject. Both students and parents are aware that things are happening differently in these subjects. Consequently, the most efficient way to change the reporting system is to add a supplemental report for these two subjects. Rather than put a math grade on the traditional report card, the teacher writes a note saying, "See supplemental report." As other subjects are individualized, the supplemental reports become the school's reporting system. In this way the change is gradual, and parents see it not as controversial or traumatic, but as logical and well planned.

When planning an individualized instructional program, put the needs of the students first.

Chapter 10
Implementing
Individualized
Instruction

In a lecture giving an overview of individualized instruction, the first transparency showed an old teacher, her white hair fixed in a bun, standing stiffly behind her desk and saying, "You'll never change me!" Forty transparencies later, the old teacher reappeared. This time she was shown walking out from behind her desk, leaning heavily on her cane and saying, "I might bend a little."

Change isn't easy. We all want change; everyone likes to have more excitement, better health, more money, more fun, more friends. At the same time, everyone wants things to stay the same: grandmother's homemade biscuits, your parents' home, old-time beer, old-time values. One emphasis of Alvin Toffler's recent book *Future Shock* is that everyone wants change; the question is how much and how fast.

A teacher who asks, "Help me individualize my classroom," or a principal who says, "Make us a nongraded school," needs to realize that such changes take time and planning. The implementation plan and in-service training program in this chapter have been used to help over forty schools make the change from traditional programs to one of the individualized models (Individually Guided Education [IGE], continuous progress, or open school). They have helped many teachers to "bend a little."

A School Implementation Plan

In interviews with teachers in schools that had just implemented individualized instruction programs, it became apparent that most of them believed in individualizing, but that they were concerned because the new program had been forced on them from "above" or because the introduction to the system "scared" them. An effective implementation plan must contain: (1) *commitment* by the district (central office), the principal, and the building staff; (2) a helpful, non-threatening *in-service training program,* and (3) *pacing* of the implementation that is based on student needs and pilot program findings.

The following sequence for implementing an individualized instructional program in a single school building can be used by the staff or faculty steering committee of an elementary or middle school. The steps in the sequence are:

1. *Self-study.* A need to improve the instructional program in the school is determined or identified. A self-study makes certain that the needs of the students are placed first. This need may be based on student test results, student performance, teacher recommendations, student interviews, parent interviews, and so on. The first step is the collection of data and the identification of student needs that are not currently being met.

2. *Study of systems for individualizing instruction.* The entire faculty or the steering committee studies available systems. This study may include attending conferences and workshops; examining reports, materials, and research findings; visiting schools that have implemented individualization; training staff in summer workshops or on-site at a fully functioning school.

3. *A system is selected (commitment).* The faculty steering committee identifies the program that is most likely to meet student needs. An overview meeting is held for the entire building staff, so that commitment can be based on appropriate knowledge and understanding of the concept. Commitment is made by the building staff and the principal. Commitment does not mean the majority of the staff voting "Yes"; it does mean consensus by the entire staff. If a teacher disagrees with the new program, she should be permitted to transfer to another building, or she should consent to accept the professional decision of her peers and try the new system.* Central office or board commitment is made, and an implementation budget is fixed. It is wise to make all commitments formal to ensure that communication has been made at all levels. At Southwest Minnesota

---

*The "We agree . . ." step presented on pages 125-26 can be used to obtain consensus.

State College, a formal commitment document includes the date that IGE was approved by the faculty, the signature of the principal, the signature of the superintendent, the date of board action, and the signature of the board president.

4. *A key person to coordinate the implementation is identified.* This person attends conferences and receives special training so that he or she can lead or assist in in-service training. Often the principal and the unit leaders receive this special training. In that case, the principal becomes the spokesman for the implementation.

5. *In-service training.* An in-service training program for the school staff members who will pilot the program is scheduled. This training should include both knowledge and application objectives. The teachers should know how the individualized system works and have an opportunity to try it for a short time with students before the new school year begins. (A more complete description of an IGE in-service training program is included on pages 115-26.)

6. *Pacing.* School staffs are encouraged to individualize in only one skill subject during the first year of implementation. They should team teach and provide learning alternatives in one content subject during the first year. The first subjects chosen should be determined by the student needs identified in the self-study. A three- to five-year plan for implementing the program in the other skill and content areas should be made.

7. *Monitoring.* The individualized instruction program is monitored throughout the school year(s).

8. *Research findings.* The data collected from the pilot school are used to determine whether to expand the program, alter it, or abandon it.

An In-Service Training Program

The in-service training program that follows has been used by the staff at Southwest Minnesota State College to help schools implement IGE. Training programs have been conducted as college courses or summer workshops at the schools and as on-campus summer workshops. The program can also be used to implement the continuous progress model or the open school model.

The program has three parts: (1) the school staff is reorganized into units and taught the skills needed in IGE; (2) the unit teams plan and pilot teach a skill unit and a content unit to demonstrate the IGE skills; and (3) the Instructional Improvement Committee

(IIC) and the unit teams evaluate the pilot teaching, build a team philosophy, and finalize implementation plans.

Before the in-service training begins, the school staff and the principal should be committed to the implementation of IGE. This commitment can be tentative, since it will be reevaluated at the end of the training program. Preferably, the program should be team taught by a member of the local school staff who has been trained in IGE and a consultant or practitioner who is experienced in IGE. The IIC should be used by the teaching team to provide feedback, direction, and emphasis for the training program.

All materials listed in the training sequence are included in the Bibliography.

IGE IN-SERVICE TRAINING SEQUENCE

Session One

A. Overview of Individualized Instruction.
   This presentation serves as an introduction to IGE and provides the learner with the concepts presented in Chapters 1 and 2 of this book.

B. Film of IGE in Action
   Best choice: *One at a Time, Together* (16 mm film)
   Alternate choice: *The IGE Learning Program* (sound filmstrip)

C. IGE Organization—Presentation and Sound Filmstrip
   The presentation should review the organizational ideas presented in Chapter 3 of this book.
   Best choice: *Organized for Learning* (sound filmstrip)
   Alternate choice: *IGE/MUS-E Organizations and Operations* (sound filmstrip)

D. Assignment
   Read *Unit Operations and Roles,* Chapters 1-3.
   Alternate assignment: View *IGE/MUS-E Roles and Responsibilities* (sound filmstrip)

E. Special Assignment for Principal
   Organize school into units; select unit leaders; assign teachers to units. The principal should confer with each teacher before final assignments are made. This task may be completed before Session One; it must be completed before Session Two.

Session Two

A. Local School Organization Plan
The principal explains the organization plan to the staff. A discussion session may follow.
B. Introduction to Team-Building Skills
Some of the problems of teaming presented in Chapter 2 of this book should be reviewed and the Joe-Harry Window should be introduced.

The Joe-Harry Window (Figure 10) illustrates in a simple way what should be accomplished in a team-building session.

The top, left box is called the "Common Knowledge Box." This knowledge includes things that both you and I know about me: I am five feet eight, have blue eyes, etc. In the bottom, left box are the things I know about myself but you don't. Some of these things are my secrets, things I'm not going to let you know; some are things I haven't had time to tell you (give me time and I will). One caution: team-building is not open, free-wheeling sensitivity training; team members cannot handle intimate personal details and work together daily.

The top, right box is the "Bad Breath Box." These are the things you can see or have discovered about me, but of which I am unaware. Below is the "Hidden Potential Box." These are the things I don't know about myself and you don't know about me either.

In a good team, the Common Knowledge Box grows larger and larger. As it expands, it dips into the Hidden Potential Box, and gradually each team member becomes more effective.

Fig. 10. The Joe-Harry Window

Things about myself that I . . .

		know	don't know
Things about myself that others . . .	know	common knowledge	my blind spots, such as bad breath, that my best friends haven't told me yet
	do not know	my secrets and things I haven't had a chance to tell yet	my hidden potential, things I never dreamed I could do or be

Adapted from "The Johari Window" in *Group Processes,* by Joseph Luft (Palo Alto, Calif.: The National Press, 1963), pp. 10-15.

The effective team has open communication, a living philosophy of education, and a helping relationship. The concept of a helping relationship is based on the notion that team members can help each other grow and increase each other's potential abilities. In a truly helping relationship, team members build more trust; and the more trust they build, the more they share and develop their potential. Trust is the key word in achieving a helping relationship.

C. The Team-Building Sequence

A model for group work that has been developed suggests four steps for helping a group work effectively: (1) getting acquainted and developing trust; (2) clarification of values; (3) identification of achievement and strengths; and (4) problem solving and goal setting.*

This model provides a pattern for the team-building sequence that follows. The activities can be led by the principal or by a workshop leader. Teams must be organized prior to the training sessions. All activities are designed to be completed within the unit team.

1. Warm-up activities. Whips are quick verbal exercises that help team members get to know each other.

   a. Proud Whip. Each team member shares with the team something she has done or something that she owns that she is particularly proud of and tells why she is proud of it.

   b. What My Name Means to Me. Each team member states her name to the team and tells what it means to her.

   c. Hero Whip. Each team member answers the question "If you could be someone else in history, movies, novels, etc., who would you be and why?"

2. Unfoldment. The workshop leader first models a personal unfoldment for the entire group. He may then direct each team member to do a personal unfoldment or a paired interview.

   a. Personal Unfoldment. The following narrative is used to introduce this exercise: "We are now going to do depth unfoldment. I will model the unfoldment process for you. I will have six minutes, as will each team member, in which to unfold in a personal way so that you will become better acquainted with who I am as a professional educator and

---

*The Group Work Model was developed in 1971 by Lowell Tornquist, Director of the Center for Applied Instruction at Southwest Minnesota State College, and has been used in workshops.

who I am as a person. During the unfoldment, each of us should share those experiences from early in life to the present moment that we feel have contributed to our being the persons we are now. These need not be traumatic experiences, but may include them. Some time during the unfoldment, perhaps during the last minute, share the peak experience of your life."

Each team should appoint a timer. If a person is unable to use the full six minutes, the team should use the remaining time to ask questions. The leader should enforce the time limit in order to accomplish the goals of the session and in order to protect a team member from taking an undue share of time and thus creating group hostility or personal anxiety. Because a positive feeling usually exists following the unfoldment, a break is recommended only if the group is very tired.[1]

b. Paired Interviews. This activity is done as follows. Choose a member of your team whom you do not know well. It is your task to find out in an interview as much about your partner as possible. Take notes, and ask any questions you wish. The person being interviewed has the right to refuse to answer any questions. After an eight- to ten-minute interview, return to the group and tell about the person you interviewed. Stand behind the person as you tell about her, and report in the first person. Then change roles and repeat the procedure. (This is an effective technique for use with teachers who know each other well.)

3. Listening Exercise. One of the skills good teaching teams must have is the ability to listen to each other. In this exercise, all team members should feed back to the first person who shared in an unfoldment or an interview report just how much they remember. The feedback should continue around the group in the order that they shared.

This exercise focuses on both listening skills and empathy. Group members may discover how well they listened or should listen. In addition, the persons who are being talked about will discover that the group already knows a lot about them.

4. Nonverbal Trust Walk (Blind). The leader directs the group to pair off in twos and asks one member of each pair to close her eyes and allow herself to be led by her partner. The pair may go out of the room and even out of the building, but they should return to the room in five to ten building, but they

should return to the room in five to ten minutes. When they return, the partners switch roles and repeat the exercise. Throughout the exercise, the partners should not talk, but rely on nonverbal communication to accomplish the guidance. A feeling of cooperation and trust is the desired outcome.

5. Values. By completing the following form, "Preferred Qualities of Children," team members become aware of their different values.

Preferred Qualities of Children*

Instructions: After reading completely through the qualities or characteristics of children, as listed below, assign number "1" to the quality which you believe would be the most desirable quality in this list for a ___-year-old child. Then assign "2" to the attribute which you regard as second most important, "3" to the third most important, and so on until you have assigned a number to all ten of those listed qualities. You may, of course, change your mind or correct any assigned numbers as you go along. Please assign a number to each of these ten attributes, even if you find it quite difficult to make some choices. No tie scores, please.

BOY   GIRL

_____ responsible and trustworthy _____ A

_____ neat and clean _____ B

_____ curious _____ C

_____ interacts well with others _____ D

_____ considerate and cooperative _____ E

_____ assertive and self-reliant _____ F

_____ able to make friends _____ G

_____ respectful toward adults _____ H

_____ fun-loving and carefree _____ I

_____ imaginative and creative _____ J

*Hurley, J.R. and Randolph, C.C. Behavioral Attributes Preferred in Eight-Year-Olds. *JSAS Catalog of Selected Documents in Psychology,* Fall, 1971, 1, 10.

When each member of the team has completed the form, team members should compare their answers freely. When all teams have compared their answers, the leader should instruct each participant to add her scores for B, E, and H (structured) and compare the total with the total for C, F, and J (unstructured). There are no right answers, but different values of team members may become apparent.

6. Helper-Helpee. This exercise truly demonstrates how an effective team functions. Each team member takes a turn at being the helpee, while the other team members serve as helpers. The helpee shares a problem with the team, such as, "I have trouble teaching phonics," or, "I'm not successful teaching boys like Billy." Then the helpers try to help her solve the problem. Adequate time should be provided for the completion of this activity.

D. Assignment
Read *IGE Learning Program* and *IGE Multiage Grouping.*

Session Three

A. Team Planning Strategies
Discussion and sound filmstrip, *IGE Planning System.*

B. Team-Building Skills—Strength Bombardment
Group participants should be getting to know a lot about each other. It is now appropriate to ask them to identify the personal strengths of the other group members. For the Strength Bombardment exercise, each team member will need a sheet of newsprint. The sheets are taped to the wall, and each one is divided into two columns (the column on the right should be only four to six inches wide). At the top of the left column is written *Strengths Others See in Me* and at the top of the right column, *Strengths I See in Myself.* The name of the person whose strengths are to be identified is written at the top of the newsprint. Next the chairs should be arranged so that each person can easily walk up to the newsprint and write. The first segment is nonverbal. The team members take turns writing the strengths of the team member on the newsprint with a felt pen. When the newsprint is filled or no one else wants to record a strength, the verbal phase begins. Each person explains why she wrote the strength she did or clarifies what the strength means. Finally, the person whose strengths have been listed stands and validates (or negates) the strengths by checking them in the column titled

Strengths I See in Myself. She also verbalizes her reasons for agreeing or disagreeing with the opinions. When she finishes, one of the team members should remove the newsprint from the wall and present it to her. The process continues until every person in the group has a record of her personal strengths.[3]

C. Team Problem Solving

The 16 mm film *The Unit Meeting* should be shown. At the first project stop, each unit team should brainstorm topics that could be taught during the pilot teaching session. The brainstorming session should last from twenty to thirty minutes and should be tape-recorded. The ideas generated should be listed on the chalkboard. After this session, the groups should resume viewing the film. The projection stops on destructive team behaviors (monopolizer, criticizer) should be reviewed only briefly. At project stop 4, the unit teams should play back the tape of the brainstorming session to see if they have a monopolizer or criticizer in the group. Then the remainder of the film should be viewed.

D. Assignment*

Read Chapter 4 in *Individualizing Instruction and Keeping Your Sanity.*

Alternate assignment: Read *IGE Assessment.*

Session Four

A. Criterion-Referenced Instruction

This presentation reviews the concepts in the first part of Chapter 4 of this book. The emphasis is on how to write behavioral objectives. Each participant may be pre-assessed to see how knowledgeable she is in this area.

Alternate or additional activity: *IGE/MUS-E Instructional Programming in IGE* (sound filmstrip).

B. The Behavioral Objective Game.

This activity provides a good pre-assessment of each team's understanding of criterion-referenced instruction.

1. Each member of the team writes a behavorial objective in a different skill or content area.
2. The objective is passed to the team member on the right, who

---

*For some school staffs, it may be appropriate for each team to complete the "We agree . . ." step on pages 125-26 at this time.

writes a pre-assessment plan for the objective. It should be emphasized that this is a plan. Sample items may be developed, but a complete pretest should not be written.

3. The objective and the pre-assessment plan are passed to the right again. The team member who receives them writes at least two diversified learning activities for teaching the objective.

4. The objective, pre-assessment plan, and learning activities are again passed to the right. This team member writes a post-assessment plan for the objective.

5. The learning program is returned to the team member who wrote the objective. The team examines all the learning programs and selects the best one.

C. Assessment Strategies

Best choice: *IGE/MUS-E Assessment in IGE* (sound filmstrip)

Alternate choice: *Performance Testing and Observation* (sound filmstrip)

Discussion should follow the audio-visual presentation.

D. Team Planning Time

Teams should be given some time to begin planning for the pilot teaching program.

E. Assignment

Read Chapters 5 and 6 in *Individualizing Instruction and Keeping Your Sanity.*

Session Five

A. Learning Styles

This presentation reviews the concepts in Chapter 5 of this book.

B. Learning Modes (Audio-Visual Presentation)

Best choice: *Learning Modes* (sound filmstrip)

Alternate choice: *IGE/MUS-E Grouping Patterns* (sound filmstrip)

C. Using the Learning Modes

This presentation reviews the one-to-one mode and the small group models.

D. Demonstration of Small Group Model

Each unit team plans a microteach, using one of the small group models. One team member goes to another unit team and teaches the model. The teams regroup and discuss the experience.

E. *Many Roads* (Optional)

This 16 mm film shows how one school uses diversified learning activities.

F. Team Planning Time (Optional)
G. Assignment
Read Chapters 7 and 8 of *Individualizing Instruction and Keeping Your Sanity.*

Session Six (This is the last input session.)

A. Writing the Content Unit (Audio-Visual Presentation)
Teaching Units and Lesson Plans (sound filmstrip)
B. Managing the IGE Learning Program
The first two filmstrips in the series *Managing the IGE Learning Environment* should be shown and discussed. (Participants may want to view the other two filmstrips in this series as well.) The emphasis in the discussion should be on record keeping and on building learning stations.
C. Team Planning Session
Unit teams should begin to delegate work for the pilot teaching.
D. Assignment
Plan for pilot teaching.

Session Seven

A. School Visitation
The participants should visit one or more functioning IGE schools. It is best if unit teams are split up so that the team members can see more than one school in action. Visitation usually gives team members both ideas and the confidence that they can individualize.
B. Assignment
Prepare for pilot teaching.

Session Eight

A. Planning for Pilot Teaching
1. Unit teams should teach from two to five half days.
a. If possible, teachers should not teach their regular students. Changing students and only teaching half days will keep both student and teacher enthusiasm for the pilot teaching high. If all teams are teaching at the same time, these should be consecutive half days. The workshop leaders should code and video-tape or audio-tape each unit team to provide objective feedback to the team members.

    b. If there are matched teams (i.e., one team teaching and one team observing), the unit teams may teach alternate days, weeks, etc.

2. Requirements. Each unit team should
    a. teach a skill unit (with pre-assessment);
    b. teach a content unit;
    c. model one or more small groups;
    d. build one or more learning stations.
3. The emphasis of the pilot teaching should be on the teachers' demonstrating the skills required in individualizing instruction. If the students learn (and they will), this is a "fringe benefit."

B. Monitoring

Each unit team should "talk through" the pilot teaching plans with a workshop leader. The leader will check to see if the plans model IGE teaching.

Session Nine

Pilot Teaching

Session Ten

A. Feedback for Pilot Teaching

Each unit identifies the strengths and weaknesses of the skill unit, the content unit, and the entire pilot teaching. Feedback from workshop leaders or matched teams should be given to each unit team. The video tapes should be viewed and discussed.

B. View 16 mm film *Tuesday*

This film provides an introduction to the daily operation of a unit team. It can help a team develop ground rules for team operation.

C. Introduce "We agree . . ."

This is the most important of the team-building skills, and each team must be given ample time to complete this activity fully. The purpose of the "We agree . . ." step is to build a living team philosophy. The words "We agree" should be written on a chalk-board or on newsprint. Then the team should generate as many statements as possible that all agree on, such as "Children learn . . ."; "The role of the teacher is . . ."; "The school should . . ."; "The student outcomes for our unit are . . .". The "We agree . . ." step helps each team member internalize the team philosophy.

A building philosophy can be developed from the "We agree . . ." statements. Each team's statements should be edited and reproduced on a transparency. Special teachers should develop "I agree" statements, which should be shared and discussed at a faculty meeting. A committee including the principal can combine the statements to form a building philosophy of education.

D. Assignment

Complete the "We agree . . ." step.

E. Party

Celebrate the successful pilot teaching!

Session Eleven (This session may be planned by the IIC.)

A. Share and discuss the "We agree . . ." statements.
B. Present implementation strategies.
  1. Which subjects will be individualized?
  2. How will students get into a unit?
  3. How will the public relations program function?

*If you want to play bridge, you don't play
alone. Trying to individualize by yourself is
just as foolish.*

Chapter 11
The League:
A Support Network
for Individualized
Instruction

Teachers and administrators who have worked in innovative school programs know that visitors can be very frustrating. Many visitors who see an effective individualized program in action become defensive and make statements such as, "I don't like your math program," or, "I don't think kids should be allowed to select their own UNIPACS," or, "It looked a little loose to me." Often they use this statement: "We do that same thing at our school, we just don't call it   (fill in the blank with a word of your own choosing—nongrading, prescriptive teaching, IGE, etc.)." Or they say, "We can't do that at our school because   (our facilities are too cramped, 'THEY' won't let us, our budget is too tight, the other staff are too traditional, etc.)."

One principal of a nongraded school became so frustrated with the negative comments of visitors that he placed a sign above the door of his office. The sign stated in bold type "I DON'T LIKE YOUR SCHOOL EITHER!"

Another principal in a large city school district gave leadership to the implementation of the pilot IGE program in the city. A visiting administrator commented to him, "I'll bet the other principals in the city are watching your program with interest." "You're right," replied the principal. "They all want me to fail."

Schools compete within school districts for the approval of the central office and for the larger share of the budget this approval might bring.

Schools compete with each other, in "one-up-manship" as well as in athletic events. "Our nongraded program is better than Brown

Street School's." "They really aren't individualizing at Roosevelt School; you ought to see our program." "Our kids' reading scores on the Stanford Achievement Test were better than theirs."

Schools have not worked together. But they can. They should. And they must!

Classroom teachers who are individualizing instruction can form associations with other teachers who are individualizing. These associations can be within a school, but they are much better if they cross school lines. If you want to play bridge, you don't play alone. Trying to individualize by yourself is just as foolish. Everyone needs the support network that a group of peers or a league can bring.

How a League Can Help a School*

There are two leagues of IGE schools in southwestern Minnesota. One league has fourteen schools; the other has eleven. "We just never realized how important the league would be," explained League Facilitator Frank Nauyokas. "Principals, unit leaders, teachers, and instructional aides need support, encouragement, new ideas, and attention while they're implementing IGE. The league has helped the schools maintain and improve their individualized programs."

"For me the league has been tremendous," said IGE Principal Al Boonstra. "It's been a system of support. It's been a source of practical ideas. It's provided leadership to improve the instructional program. It's prodding me to do more. You know, without a league, a school can change and become stagnant again."

A league is an association of schools that are implementing individualized instruction. The purpose of the league is to improve the instructional program in each school. A league helps a school implement an individualized program in many ways.

1. *The league is a source of peer support.* Changing from a traditional program to an individualized program is hard work. It can be lonely and frustrating. Who does a primary unit leader in an IGE school talk to when she wants feedback or support? If she is the only primary unit leader in the school, she may spend the year talking to herself. All staff members need peer support while they

---

*Many of the ideas in this section are based on the work of Dr. Mary M. Bentzen presented in a speech at the IGE League Facilitators Meeting in Dayton, Ohio, in January, 1971, and on the book *IGE League Handbook* (Dayton, Ohio: Institute for Development of Educational Activities, 1971), pp. 2-6.

are implementing an individualized instruction program. The principal, the unit leaders, the unit teachers, the special teachers, and the instructional aides all need support.

The league breaks down communication barriers. At early league meetings, members tend to "show and tell" as a way of impressing each other. Later, the "show and tell" stage ends, and members begin to share their real concerns. League meetings provide frequent opportunities for face-to-face contacts. At these meetings, classroom problems are solved, techniques are shared, curriculum materials are reviewed, procedures are described, and friends are made. As one teacher said, "It's helpful to know that you're not the only one who's having problems individualizing."

2. *The league is a source of outside ideas.* There is a danger that a school can become self-contained. Ideas are needed from outside the school. The league provides a system for the exchange of information, techniques, and experiences. It is like team teaching on a larger scale. League members not only are bombarded with new ideas; they are also motivated to try them out.

3. *The league serves as a clearing house to identify resource people.* Every school has teachers whose expertise other schools may need. For example, a teacher who has developed a number of science UNIPACS can be a great help to unit team members trying to package their science curriculum. Like the student who helps a younger student, the league member who serves as an internal consultant improves both his self-concept and his expertise. The use of internal consultants is a process that can improve the instructional program in all the league schools.

4. *The league can legitimize school change.* Like an athletic league, a league of individualized schools can present ideas, policies, and programs to boards of education, other schools, parent groups, or citizens' groups. There is strength in numbers. The league can be a strong force for educational change. With league support, member schools can risk more and can try out more innovations.

5. *The league provides status for its members.* Individualizing instruction is challenging and innovative. Publicity and league meetings help league teachers and administrators develop an *esprit de corps.* Members are proud to belong to the league. Professional and social friendships develop. League members become a special group of persons striving for excellence in their school programs.

6. *The league provides a structure for the identification and solution of problems.* This is the most important reason for having a

league. Identifying problems and solving them are the means for improving schools. The league can provide information and resource people and can help a school see a problem objectively and solve it.

How a League Works

A league begins with an intermediate agency. An intermediate agency can be a college, a state department, a large school district, or a research council. The intermediate agency agrees to help a group of schools implement an individualized instruction program. The league of schools is centered around the intermediate agency. In southwestern Minnesota, a college and a research council have joined together to form an intermediate agency.

A league usually includes from ten to fiteen schools that are implementing individualized instruction programs. The league schools should have a fairly close geographic location, although leagues in both Minnesota and Colorado have functioned well with some members driving over one hundred miles to league meetings. It is best if the size of the league is under fifteen schools and if the schools are close enough together for contact of members to be frequent.

The intermediate agency appoints a league facilitator. This person should have a background in elementary education and be able to determine whether the components of individualized instruction are being practiced. In the IGE programs in Minnesota, there are four facilitators; two have been IGE principals, and two have been IGE unit leaders. Their experiences enable them to help school staffs that are implementing IGE programs.

It is important to recognize the distinctive role of the facilitator. His role is to facilitate. He is not an expert himself; rather, he helps the school find expertise. His responsibilities are (1) to identify and recruit schools to be part of the league; (2) to help train personnel in each league school; (3) to establish and coordinate the functions of a league; (4) to assist schools to implement individualized instruction; and (5) to develop a system for retrieving data pertaining to resource people, curricular materials, and hardware for the implementation of individualized instruction.[1]

Each league elects a hub committee to guide the operation of the league activities. This steering committee plans league activities, assists in communication, and provides feedback for the league facilitator. The hub committee is usually composed of two principals, two unit leaders, two teachers, and the league facilitator.

There are expenses connected with operating a league of cooperating schools. The facilitator's salary, office, travel, and supplies must be maintained. It costs to hold league meetings. Some leagues charge a membership fee. Some intermediate agencies, such as a state department of education, will provide these services at little or no cost to cooperating schools.

What a League Does

The purpose of a league is to improve the instructional program in each school. To do this, league activities should elicit peer support, circulate ideas, identify resource people, provide status for league members, identify problems, and offer solutions. To achieve these goals, all persons within the league must be involved. Face-to-face interaction is the most important league activity.

The league helps member schools in the following ways:

1. *Meetings* are planned frequently so that principals, unit leaders, unit teachers, special teachers, and instructional aides can communicate. There are three types of meetings: total league meetings, sub-group meetings, and in-service meetings.

Total league meetings for all personnel are held two to four times each year. These meetings usually offer social activities, role-alike sessions, and a smorgasbord of interest sessions.

Sub-group meetings for principals, unit leaders, unit teachers, and instructional aides are held regularly. Monthly meetings are held for the principals. The other groups meet two to six times a year.

In-service meetings are planned by the hub committee and are held frequently. In southwestern Minnesota, topics for in-service meetings have included learning stations, evaluation, the Wisconsin Reading Design, Individualized Mathematics Study, and management strategies. League members can select and attend any or all of the in-service meetings.

2. *Teacher visitation and teacher exchange* can be provided within the league. Teachers can visit and observe in other league schools. League members can exchange roles for a short period of time. Teacher exchange is an excellent way to learn how to use new techniques or materials. "Teachers who try teacher exchange are very positive," reported League Facilitator Frank Nauyokas, "but it's like pulling teeth to get them to try it."

3. The league can provide *consultant help*. Once a school

identifies a problem, the league can help the school find help in solving the problem. If a resource person is needed, the league can facilitate visits of consultants, either from within the league or from outside it.

4. A *resource file* can be provided by the league. This file contains both lists and materials. A catalog of resource personnel, in-service training materials, and curriculum materials is made available to all league members. Suggestions on how the in-service materials can be obtained or which curriculum materials are appropriate for individualized instruction are included in the catalog.

5. A *monthly newsletter* is published by the league facilitator. News from the league schools, new ideas, league members' successes, a calendar of events, and school needs are included in the newsletter. The newsletter makes a formal presentation of what the league schools are accomplishing.

The above are but a few of the ways that a league can help a school. Most of all, the league helps by giving each member support, encouragement, and new ideas. The great thing about the league concept is that it really works; it really helps a teacher individualize instruction.

If a League's Not Available, Start One!

"All this stuff about leagues of cooperating schools is very interesting," said the teacher, "but what about me, trying to individualize in my self-contained classroom? I can't start my own league."

"Why not?" responded the university professor. "A group of principals in South Dakota talked Dakota State College and the state department of education into becoming an intermediate agency. Why can't you get a league started?"

"I don't know how."

"Certainly, you do," said the professor. "Just get the teachers in your school and in other schools who are trying to individualize instruction to meet to talk about needs and problems. The league can start from there."

"We'll need a facilitator," stated the teacher. "Will you be willing to serve in that role?"

The professor's face reddened. "Well . . ."

Appendix 1
Performance
Objectives Cluster

All schools operate on the basis that there are certain educational goals for their students to achieve. Often these goals are stated in terms so general or vague that they are not useful to the teacher in the classroom. To be a teacher in an individualized school system, one must learn to recognize, to write, and to use performance (behavioral) objectives. This is step one in the Southwest Minnesota State College instructional model. When objectives are sharply focused, they provide the teacher with a sense of purpose and direction and with a structure for selecting materials and procedures. Recognizing, writing, and using performance objectives are early competencies a teacher should demonstrate.

Knowledge Competencies

1. Given a list of objectives, the learner will be able to identify, with 85 percent accuracy, those that fit the criteria of a behavioral objective.

2. The learner will be able to write measurable behavioral objectives in the lower and higher level cognitive domain, in the psychomotor domain, and in the affective domain.

Application Competencies

1. After observing a student, the learner will write an appropriate objective to teach the student a specific task.

2. After developing a behavioral objective and a teaching sequence, the learner will teach the behavioral objective to peers in a microteach or to a student in a public school.

Affective Competency

After she is employed as a teacher, the learner will use the instructional management model as the basis for organizing her instructional program.

Treatment: Route to Competencies

The pre-service teacher may choose from a series of competency packages (compacs) or reading material to gain knowledge competencies. She may complete Application Competency 1 during the school visitations in Block 1. Application Competency 2 may be completed on campus, in a public school, or both.

For Knowledge Competency 1, complete Compac A 1.0111 or read *Preparing Instructional Objectives* by Robert Mager.

For Knowledge Competency 2, complete Compac A 1.0112 or

read *Establishing Instructional Goals* by James Popham and Eva Baker.

For Application Competency 1, complete Compac A 1.0113 during a field visitation.

For Application Competency 2, complete Compacs A 1.0114, A 1.0115, etc. (The amount of practice required by each pre-service teacher will vary.)

Evaluation

The knowledge competencies are evaluated by tests and an oral explanation of written materials. Application Competency 1 is evaluated during an oral interview with an evaluator. Application Competency 2 is evaluated as the learner and an evaluator study a video tape of the teaching incident. The affective competency will be measured in a follow-up study of Southwest Minnesota State College graduates.

Quest

Use one or more of the following to study performance objectives as used in a total system or in a specific discipline.

1. Study the *Wisconsin Reading Design* (Curriculum Library).

2. Study one or more of the collections of behavioral objectives developed by Instructional Objectives Exchange (Curriculum Library).

3. Read any one of the following materials from the Behavioral Objectives Extension Service (Chicago: Science Research Associates, 1969).

Behavioral Objectives and Teacher Success
Behavioral Objectives in English and Literature
Behavioral Objectives in Social Science
Behavioral Objectives in Science
Behavioral Objectives in Biology
Behavioral Objectives in Mathematics
Behavioral Objectives in Art and Music

4. Complete Compac A 1.0130, Use of Behavioral Objectives— Pros and Cons.

Compac A 1.0111   **Stating Objectives in Behavioral Terms**

Context   *Specify Educational Outcomes Desired*

Major Subject   *Educational Objectives*

Topic   *Stating Objectives in Behavioral Terms*

Target Population   *Pre-Service and In-Service Elementary*

                                     and Secondary

Behavioral Objectives

1. Given a set of objectives, the learner will select those that are measurable by identifying in each the following elements:
   a statement of the task the student will perform
   a description of the conditions under which the student will
      be required to perform the task
   the acceptable level of performance
   2. Given a description of teaching tasks and sources of information, the learner will write measurable behavioral objectives.

Prerequisite

None is required.

Pretest

No pretest is required for pre-service teachers.
   For in-service teachers who are familiar with the concepts of behavioral objectives, an evaluator (from the Center for the Management of Educational Systems) will conduct an interview with the learner before this compac is begun. If the evaluator feels that the learner understands the area covered in this compac, he will instruct the learner to take the self-test on pages 56-60 of *Preparing Instructional Objectives* by Robert Mager. If the learner misses five or fewer items on the test, she may exit this compac.

Treatment

   1. Read *Preparing Instructional Objectives* by Robert Mager.
   2. View the filmstrip/cassette set *Systematic Instructional Decision-Making* (VIMCET #55). Write the answer as you view.
   3. View *Educational Objectives* (VIMCET #54) and write the answer as you view.

4. Read "Nature and Function of Educational Objectives" on pages 113-25 in *Modern Elementary Curriculum* by W. B. Ragan.

As an alternate plan for Objective 1, view, with an overhead projector, the transparency set on behavioral objectives available in the lab.

For Objective 2 (elementary), write five behavioral objectives for the following teaching situations:

1. teaching directions on a wall map
2. teaching kindergarten children to identify five colors
3. teaching primary children to regroup (borrow) in subtraction.

For Objective 2 (secondary), write five behavioral objectives in your own discipline.

Materials

Mager, Robert. *Preparing Instructional Objectives.* Palo Alto, Calif.: Fearon Publishers, 1962.

Ragan, W. B. *Modern Elementary Curriculum.* New York: Holt, Rinehart & Winston, 1966.

Educational Objectives. (VIMCET #54) A filmstrip/cassette set.
Systematic Instructional Decision-Making. (VIMCET #55) A film-strip/cassette set.

Filmstrip viewer and cassette recorder
Overhead projector and Behavioral Objectives transparencies

Evaluation

After you have written five behavioral objectives, show them to a faculty member (Center for the Management of Educational Systems).

Quest

This is to be initiated by learner.

Compac A 1.0112   Writing Behavioral Objectives in the Cognitive, Affective, and Psychomotor Domains

Context   *Specify Educational Outcomes Desired*

Major Subject   *Educational Objectives*

Topic   *Writing Behavioral Objectives*

Target Population   *Pre-Service and In-Service Elementary and Secondary*

Behavioral Objectives

1. The learner will name and define the three domains of learning.

2. The learner will identify written objectives representing the cognitive, affective, and psychomotor domains of student behavior.

3. Having properly identified cognitive behavioral objectives, the learner will be able to classify them as (a) lower or (b) higher than the lowest level in the cognitive domain.

4. Given a specific cognitive teaching task, the learner will write two measurable behavioral objectives.

5. Given a specific affective teaching task, the learner will write two measurable behavioral objectives.

6. Given a specific psychomotor teaching task, the learner will write two measurable behavioral objectives.

Prerequisite

Complete Compac A 1.0111, Stating Objectives in Behavioral Terms.

Pretest

A discussion will be held between the learner and a member of the faculty of the Center for the Management of Educational Systems. If the learner demonstrates a knowledge of the cognitive, affective, and psychomotor domains and can identify behavioral objectives in each of these domains, she may bypass Objectives 1, 2, and 3. (A self-test for Objectives 1, 2, and 3 is available in the Education Learning Center.)

Treatment

For Objectives 1 and 2, view the filmstrip/cassette set *Selecting*

Appropriate Educational Objectives (VIMCET #56). Write the answers as you view.

For Objective 3, view the filmstrip/cassette set *Defining Content for Objectives* (VIMCET #62) and write your answers on your own paper.

For Objectives 4, 5, and 6, write two behavioral objectives in the cognitive domain—one lower and one higher; two in the affective domain; and two in the psychomotor domain. For secondary, write your objectives in your own discipline. For elementary, choose from the following list of specific teaching tasks.

1. teaching use of tools in the woodshop
2. teaching the types of housing used by Indians
3. teaching uses of the corn crop in Minnesota
4. teaching use of the tape recorder
5. teaching an appreciation of music by Chopin
6. teaching gymnastic stunts
7. teaching an appreciation of watercolor paintings
8. teaching popcorn making
9. teaching the spelling of words ending in *-ment*
10. teaching the color wheel

Materials

Defining Content for Objectives (VIMCET #62) a filmstrip/cassette set. (available on compac shelf)
Selecting Appropriate Educational Objectives (VIMCET #56) a filmstrip/cassette set. (available on compac shelf)

Filmstrip viewer and cassette recorder

Evaluation

Take the two-page test covering Objectives 1, 2, and 3. Check it against the key. If you miss two or more items, discuss the results with an evaluator.

For Objectives 4, 5, and 6, after you have written at least six behavioral objectives from the teaching situations listed or from your discipline, show your written work to an evaluator. Turn in the objectives to be checked and filed.

Compac A 1.0113	**Writing Behavioral Objectives for a Specific Teaching Task**
Context	*Specify Educational Outcomes Desired*
Major Subject	*Educational Objectives*
Topic	*Writing Behavioral Objectives for a Specific Teaching Task*
Target Population	*Pre-Service and In-Service Elementary and Secondary*

Behavioral Objective

The learner will write an appropriate behavioral objective to teach a specific student a specific task.

Prerequisite

Complete Compac A 1.0112, Writing Behavioral Objectives in the Cognitive, Affective, and Psychomotor Domains.

Pretest

Since this compac requires demonstration skill, no pretest is available.

Treatment

Observe one student having learning problems defined by the classroom teacher. In a written report, describe the student, identify and describe the learning difficulty, and write behavioral objectives to teach the specific task necessary to resolve the learning difficulty. Give your reasoning for choosing your objectives. Make certain your objectives are in behavioral terms as suggested in Compacs A 1.0111 and A 1.0112.

Materials

Classroom observation time

Evaluation

Present a written report to an evaluator. Be prepared to discuss it.

Quest

This is to be initiated by the learner. Writing behavioral objectives for another learner is a possibility.

Compac A 1.0114   **Teaching a Behavioral Objective**

Context   *Determining Educational Outcomes*

Major Subject   *Behavioral Objectives*

Topic   *Teaching a Behavioral Objective*

Target Population   *Pre-Service and In-Service Elementary*

                             and Secondary

Behavioral Objectives

1. The learner will write a behavioral objective relating to a specific student or group of students and have it approved by an evaluator.

2. Using audio or video tape, the learner will organize and manage an episode with a student or group of students. The learner will specifically name a desired behavior to be exhibited by the student(s) at the conclusion of the episode.

3. With an evaluator, the learner will judge her success by listening to her tape and determining if the students actually displayed the desired behavior.

Prerequisite

Complete Compac A 1.0113, Writing Behavioral Objectives for a Specific Teaching Task.

Treatment

For Objective 1, write and briefly plan a short lesson for a specific group of students, who can be children or adults. The lesson should be appropriate to the level, interest, and maturity of the group. Secondary teachers should plan to work in their major area. Your objective may be in the cognitive, affective, or psychomotor domain. Have the objective approved by an evaluator before you plan to teach your lesson.

For Objectives 2 and 3, plan to use either audio or video taping equipment to record your lesson. Your choice may depend upon what is available and what seems most appropriate to your lesson. For example, an objective that calls for students to speak could best be done with audio tape; an objective that asks the students to do something may require video tape. Be sure that you provide all materials for your lesson. Make your lesson short—five minutes may be enough. If writing is required by the students, keep their work until the evaluation session. If an evaluator can be present during your teaching session, the evaluation session could take place immediately following your lesson.

Materials

A student or group of students
Audio or video tape equipment
Necessary materials for the lesson

Evaluation

For Objective 1, have your behavioral objective approved by an evaluator prior to teaching your lesson.

For Objectives 2 and 3, sit with an evaluator to determine your success. Bring with you the results of your lesson, including any tapes and papers. Credit is obtained if your student(s) actually displayed the behavior stated in your objective.

Quest

Complete a compac dealing with teaching a behavioral objective in a specific subject or area.

Appendix 2
School
Organization
Cluster

Schools must be organized to provide each student with an individualized, personalized, humanized school program. The competent elementary teacher must have a foundation of knowledge about school organization. The teacher should demonstrate that she has the skills to teach in an Individually Guided Education (IGE) school; a Continuous Progress, or Nongraded, school; or the British Infant School. It is assumed that a pre-service teacher who has demonstrated skill in teaching in one of these models is also competent to teach in a traditional elementary school.

Knowledge Competencies

1. The learner will be able to define and give examples of vertical and horizontal patterns of school organization.
2. The learner will be able to identify the strengths and weaknesses of (a) the self-contained, graded classroom and (b) ability grouping.
3. The learner will be able to define and write a rationale for (a) nongrading, (b) team teaching, (c) multi-age grouping, and (d) differentiated staffing.
4. The learner will describe the organization of the multi-unit elementary school and explain how this structure provides for shared decision making and formal communication.

Application Competencies

1. After completing a series of team-building skills, the learner will demonstrate that she can work as a member of a unit team that plans an instructional program.
2. The learner will demonstrate that she can develop a diagnostic-prescriptive program, pre-assess students, select materials and teaching strategies, and teach an IGE learning program in both a skill subject and a content subject.

Affective Competencies

1. The learner will accept IGE; the Continuous Progress, or Nongraded, model; or the British Infant School model as better ways to organize elementary schools.
2. The pre-service teacher, once employed or as a parent, will provide active leadership to help schools change from self-contained, graded programs to more effective organizations.

Treatment: Route to Competencies

The pre-service elementary teacher may choose from a series of compacs, seminars, readings, and school visitations to gain the knowledge competencies. Once she has completed Knowledge Competencies 1, 2, and 3 and her prescriptive field experience, she should enroll in the IGE teaching sequence so that she can demonstrate the application competencies.

For Knowledge Competency 1, complete Compac E 4.0401, Classroom Organization in the Elementary School.

For Knowledge Competency 2, complete Compac E 4.0404, the Self-Contained Classroom.

For Knowledge Competency 3, do the following:

1. Complete Compac E 4.0402, A Rationale for the Nongraded School, or write a book report on *Nongraded Elementary School* by John I. Goodlad and Robert H. Anderson.

2. Complete Compac E 4.0421, Team Teaching, or E 6.0421, Team Teaching Seminar, or write a book report on any of the books listed in the "Quest" section of Compac E 4.0421.

3. Complete Compac E 4.0403, Multi-Age Grouping, or attend E 6.0403, Multi-Age Seminar.

4. Complete Compac E 4.0405, Differentiated Staffing.

Knowledge Objective 4 and Application Objectives 1 and 2 are completed in the IGE training sequence. In this program, pre-service teachers go through a sequence of team-building skills and become a unit team. The unit team observes in a school and plans and teaches IGE units in skill and content areas for a multi-age group of children. Both the skill and content units must be filed with the IGE trainer to complete this competency sequence.

Evaluation

Knowledge Competencies 1, 2, and 3 are evaluated by tests and an oral explanation of written materials. Knowledge Competency 4 is evaluated on campus during the IGE training sequence. The application competencies are demonstrated in the school during the teaching part of the IGE training sequence. The affective competencies will be measured in a follow-up study of Southwest Minnesota State College graduates.

Quest

Use one or more of the following to study other school organizational patterns. The items marked with an asterisk are included in the IGE training sequence and recommended for study there.

E 4.0406, Continuous Progress Education

E 4.0407, British Infant School (or read *Children Come First: Inspired Work of English Primary Schools* by Casey and Liza

Murrow; *Crisis in the Classroom: The Remaking in American Education* by Charles E. Silberman; or attend the seminar British Primary School—A Visitor's Report.)

*E 4.0422, Team Teaching in the Multi-Unit School
*E 4.0431, Multi-Unit School
*E 4.0432, The IGE Learning Program
*E 4.0433, Managing IGE

Compac E 4.0401   **Classroom Organization in the Elementary**

                         School

Context   *Organization and Management of the*

                         Learning Environment

Major Subject   *School Organization*

Topic   *Classroom Organization in the Elementary*

                         School

Target Population   *Pre-Service and In-Service Elementary*

Behavioral Objectives

1. The learner will be able to define vertical organizations and horizontal organizations.

2. The learner will visit a school, observe the vertical and horizontal organizational patterns, and write her observations; or the learner will reflect on the elementary school she attended and write her observations.

3. The learner will trace the development of the graded school organization.

4. The learner will identify and define plans of school organization.

Prerequisite

None is required.

Pretest

A pretest is available in the Education Learning Center.

Treatment

To identify vertical and horizontal organization for Objectives 1 and 2, read chapter 5 of *Modern Elementary Curriculum* by W. B. Ragan, *Teaching in a World of Change* by Robert H. Anderson, and chapter 12 of *Elementary Education: Today and Tomorrow* by J. Murray and Myrtle Lee. For a review or a clearer understanding of vertical and horizontal organization, listen to "Vertical and Horizontal Organization," a tape by John Goodlad (on the compac support shelf).

For Objective 3, read chapter 2 of *Individualizing Instruction and Keeping Your Sanity* by William Bechtol.

For Objective 4, read chapter 5 of *Modern Elementary Curriculum* by W. B. Ragan for information concerning IGE, British Infant Schools, and Free Schools.

Materials

Anderson, Robert H. *Teaching in a World of Change.* New York: Harcourt, Brace & World, 1966.

Bechtol, William. *Individualizing Instruction and Keeping Your Sanity.* Chicago: Follett Publishing Co., 1973.

Lee, J. Murray, and Lee, Myrtle. *Elementary Education: Today and Tomorrow.* Boston: Allyn & Bacon, 1968.

Ragan, W. B. *Modern Elementary Curriculum.* 4th ed. New York: Holt, Rinehart & Winston, 1971.

"Vertical and Horizontal Organization." A tape by John Goodlad.

Evaluation

For Objectives 1, 3, and 4, the learner will take the post-test, have a paraprofessional correct it, and discuss it with an instructor.

For Objective 2, the learner will discuss her written observation of school organizational patterns with an instructor.

Quest

Choose and study two or more compacs on school organization (4.0400 series).

Compac E 4.0404	The Self-Contained Classroom
Context	*Organization and Management of the Learning Environment*
Major Subject	*School Organization*
Topic	*The Self-Contained Classroom*
Target Population	*Pre-Service and In-Service Elementary*

Behavioral Objectives

1. The learner will define and describe briefly, in writing, ability (homogeneous) grouping, heterogeneous grouping, criterion-referenced teaching, interest grouping, and departmentalization.
2. The learner will list four advantages and four disadvantages of homogeneous grouping.
3. The learner will define and describe the self-contained classroom.
4. The learner will list four strengths and three weaknesses of the self-contained classroom.
5. In an essay test, the learner will demonstrate understanding of the concepts of ability grouping and the self-contained classroom by developing solutions or analyses of four described situations.

Prerequisite

Complete Compac E 4.0401, Classroom Organization in the Elementary School.

Treatment

All the following readings are necessary to achieve Objectives 1-5.
1. chapter 5 of *Modern Elementary Curriculum* (1971 edition) by W. B. Ragan (on shelf E 4.0401)
2. "Ability, Partial Ability and Homogeneous Grouping," pages 49-67, and "What Does Ability Grouping Do to the Self Concept," pages 80-85, in *Change and Innovation in Elementary School Organization* by M. Hillson and R. Karlson (on shelf E 4.0403)
3. pages 33-36 in *Teaching in a World of Change* by Robert Anderson (on shelf E 4.0402)
4. pages 560-62 in *Encyclopedia of Educational Research*
5. chapter 4 and chapter 7 in *Individualizing Instruction and Keeping Your Sanity* by William Bechtol

Materials

Anderson, Robert H. *Teaching in a World of Change.* New York: Harcourt, Brace & World, 1966.

Bechtol, William. *Individualizing Instruction and Keeping Your Sanity.* Chicago: Follett Publishing Co., 1973.

Ebel, Robert L., ed. *Encyclopedia of Educational Research.* 4th ed. Toronto: Macmillan Co., Collier-Macmillan, 1969.

Hillson, M., and Karlson, R., eds. *Change and Innovation in Elementary School Organization.* New York: Holt, Rinehart & Winston, 1967.

Ragan, W. B. *Modern Elementary Curriculum.* 4th ed. New York: Holt, Rinehart & Winston, 1971.

Evaluation

For Objectives 1, 2, 3, and 4, the learner will complete the tasks in writing and submit them to an evaluator.

For Objective 5, the learner will request the post-test, which will be checked by the evaluator. The learner must be able to support all answers by referring back to the readings.

Compac E 4.0402   **A Rationale for the Nongraded School**

Context   *Organization and Management of the*

                            Learning Environment

Major Subject   *School Organization*

Topic   *A Rationale for the Nongraded School*

Target Population   *Pre-Service and In-Service Elementary*

Behavioral Objectives

1. The learner will answer, with 90 percent accuracy, a list of multiple choice questions that concludes that students the same age or in the same grade perform quite differently.

2. The learner will list four organizational policies of the graded school that do not provide for individual differences of children.

3. The learner will answer, with 90 percent accuracy, multiple choice questions that conclude that non-promotion does not improve learning or a child's self-image.

4. Given a list of items, the learner will identify correctly those that are basic assumptions of the nongraded organization.

5. The learner, assuming the role of a classroom teacher, will develop a rationale (a statement, exposition, or explanation of reasons or principles) to explain to parents why a school is changing from a graded organization to a nongraded organization.

Prerequisite

Complete Compac E 4.0401, Classroom Organization in the Elementary School.

Treatment

For Objective 1, read pages 1-29 in *Nongraded Elementary School* by John I. Goodlad and Robert H. Anderson. Then, in a classroom, observe the range of performance demonstrated by children of the same age and grade level, discuss this with the teacher, and write a brief summary of your observation and discussion to be filed as part of the evaluation of this compac. List three reasons that children of the same age and grade level do not learn school subjects in the same way. Finally, view a video tape or attend a seminar on nongraded classroom organization.

For Objective 2, read chapter 2 of *Individualizing Instruction and Keeping Your Sanity* by William Bechtol and pages 58-59 of

Nongraded Elementary School. List four organizational policies of the graded school that do not provide for individual differences of children.

For Objective 3, read chapter 2 of *Nongraded Elementary School* and pages 393-402 of *The Elementary School.*

For Objective 4, view the film *Charlie and the Golden Hamster* (in the film rack) and view and listen to the filmstrip/record sets *Nongraded Education: An Overview* and *Effecting the Change to a Nongraded Program.* Also, read pages 52-58 in *Nongraded Elementary School* by Goodlad and Anderson and pages 45-70 in *Teaching in a World of Change* by Robert H. Anderson.

For Objective 5, use the reading you have done and the understanding you have gained from it to write briefly, from the role of a classroom teacher, a rationale to explain to parents why your school is changing from a graded organization to a nongraded organization.

Materials

Anderson, Robert H. *Teaching in a World of Change.* New York: Harcourt, Brace & World, 1966.
Bechtol, William. *Individualizing Instruction and Keeping Your Sanity.* Chicago: Follett Publishing Co., 1973.
Goodlad, John I., and Anderson, Robert H. *Nongraded Elementary School.* New York: Harcourt, Brace & World, 1959.
Herrick, Goodlad, et al. *The Elementary School.* Englewood Cliffs, N.J.: Prentice-Hall, 1956.

Charlie and the Golden Hamster—The Nongraded Elementary School. Film. Dayton, Ohio: Institute for Development of Educational Activities, 1970.
Effecting the Change to a Nongraded Program. Filmstrip and record. Jamaica, N.Y.: Eye Gate House.
Nongraded Education: An Overview. (#197-A) Filmstrip and record. Jamaica, N.Y.: Eye Gate House.

Filmstrip Projector
Phonograph

Evaluation

Take the post-test; have it checked by an aide (any instructor in the Division of Education). Test will include Objectives 1, 2, 3, and 4; 90 percent accuracy is required.

For Objective 1, the learner will also submit to an evaluator the written summary of a classroom observation and the list of three reasons that children do not learn in the same way. For Objective 2, the learner will submit the written list of four organizational policies.

Include in the paragraphs you write for Objective 5 three reasons that explain the rationale of the nongraded school. Discuss your work with an instructor.

For the learner who would like to study further the nongraded school organization, Dr. John Goodlad has developed three theoretical models:

1. Model A—the graded school
2. Model B—the school moving toward nongrading
3. Model C—the child-centered nongraded school

Listen to the tape "Models" by Dr. Goodlad (on the compac support shelves).

Read and work through the instructional package *Nongrading— How It Looks in the Real World* by Sue Warren and Fred Rohde.

Compac E 4.0421	**Team Teaching**
Context	*Organization and Management of the*
	Learning Environment
Major Subject	*Classroom Organization*
Topic	*Team Teaching*
Target Population	*Pre-Service and In-Service Elementary*
	and Secondary

Behavioral Objectives

1. The learner will be able to write a definition of team teaching.

2. The learner will be able to identify the characteristics of a team-teaching organization.

3. The learner will observe a film on a cooperative teaching program and identify the characteristics of team teaching exhibited in the film.

4. The learner will write a rationale for team teaching and describe the student population and the make-up of her ideal team.

Treatment

For an overview, view the filmstrip *Organized for Learning* (on shelf E 4.0431).

For Objectives 1 and 2, read the following supplementary articles: "Team Teaching," "Characteristics of Team Teaching," "Teaching in Teams," "Initial Steps in Establishing Team Teaching," "A Team Project," "Team Teaching," and "Theory and Practice in Team Teaching." Then write a definition of team teaching in your own words.

For Objective 3, view the film *Team Teaching in the Elementary School.*

For Objective 4, read chapter 3 of *Individualizing Instruction and Keeping Your Sanity* by William Bechtol.

Materials

Anderson, Robert H. "Theory and Practice in Team Teaching" in *Teaching in a World of Change.* New York: Harcourt, Brace & World, 1966.

Bechtol, William. *Individualizing Instruction and Keeping Your Sanity.* Chicago: Follett Publishing Co., 1973.

"Characteristics of Team Teaching." Dayton, Ohio: Institute for Development of Educational Activities.

Dufay, Frank. "A Team Project" in *Ungrading the Elementary School.* West Nyack, N.Y.: Parker Publishing, 1966.

Educational Facilities Laboratory. *Schools for Team Teaching.* page 65. New York: 1961.

Evans and Clinch. "Teaching in Teams."

Ragan, W. B. "Team Teaching" in *Modern Elementary Curriculum.* pages 145-47 in 1960 ed. and pages 146-49 in 1971 ed. New York: Holt, Rinehart & Winston.

"Team Teaching." *National Elementary School Principal.*

White, Darrell K. "Initial Steps in Establishing Team Teaching" in *Team Teaching.* Weber School District, November 1966.

Team Teaching in the Elementary School. Film. Dayton, Ohio: Institute for Development of Educational Activities.

Organized for Learning. Filmstrip and tape. Dayton, Ohio: Institute for Development of Educational Activities.

Evaluation

For Objective 1, write a brief definition of team teaching in your own words.

For Objectives 2 and 3, identify and describe, in writing, six or more characteristics of team teaching.

For Objective 4, present, in writing, your rationale for team teaching. Be prepared to defend it.

Quest

Prearrange with your advisor to study team teaching in greater depth. The following books provide a working bibliography.

Bair, Medill, and Woodward, Richard G. *Team Teaching in Action.* Boston: Houghton Mifflin Co., 1964.

Chamberlin, Leslie. *Team Teaching, Organization and Administration.* Columbus, Ohio: Charles E. Merrill Publishing Co., 1969.

Hanslovsky, Glenda; Mayer, Sue; and Wagner, Helen. *Why Team Teaching.* Columbus, Ohio: Charles E. Merrill Publishing Co., 1969.

Lobb, M. Delbert. *Practical Aspects of Team Teaching.* Palo Alto, Calif.: Fearon Publishers, 1964.

York, Jean L. *The Roles of the Professional and Paraprofessional Personnel in Team Teaching.* Team Teaching Modules, vol. 2. Dallas: Leslie Press, 1971.

———. *Materials and Resources Needed for Team Teaching and Individualized Instruction.* Team Teaching Modules, vol. 3. Dallas: Leslie Press, 1971.
———. *Grouping Children for Instruction in Team Teaching.* Team Teaching Modules, vol. 4. Dallas: Leslie Press, 1971.
———. *Team Teaching as a Facilitator of the Nongraded School.* Team Teaching Modules, vol. 5. Dallas: Leslie Press, 1971.
———. *Evaluation of Team Teaching and Children's Continuous Progress.* Team Teaching Modules, vol. 6. Dallas: Leslie Press, 1971.
———. *Prerequisites for Good Planning Sessions in Team Teaching.* Team Teaching Modules, vol. 7. Dallas: Leslie Press, 1971.

Compac E 4.0403   **Multi-Age Grouping**

Context   *Organization and Management of the*

                             Learning Environment

Major Subject   *School Organization*

Topic   *Multi-Age Grouping*

Target Population   *Pre-Service and In-Service Elementary*

Behavioral Objectives

1. The learner will define and describe multi-age grouping.
    2. The learner will write an essay that includes the advantages of multi-age grouping for the student and for the classroom teacher (or for the teaching team).

Pretest

There is no pretest, as this is a choice compac.

Prerequisite

Complete Compac E 4.0401, Classroom Organization in the Elementary School.

Treatment

For Objectives 1 and 2, read the following material:
    1. chapter 2 of *Individualizing Instruction and Keeping Your Sanity* by William Bechtol
    2. *IGE Multiage Grouping* (on shelf)
    3. "The Multiage-Multigraded Organization" by Doris Olson
    4. chapter 3, pages 58-70, of *The Children Come First: Inspired Work of English Primary Schools* by Casey and Liza Murrow (on shelf)
    5. "Dual Progress and Multiage or Multigrade Grouping Plans," pages 244-49, and "By Their Differences They Learn," pages 279-84, in *Change and Innovation in Elementary School Organization.*

Materials

Bechtol, William. *Individualizing Instruction and Keeping Your Sanity.* Chicago: Follett Publishing Co., 1973.

Hillson, M. and Karlson, R., eds. *Change and Innovation in Elementary School Organization.* New York: Holt, Rinehart & Winston, 1967.

Institute for Development of Educational Activities. *IGE Multiage Grouping.* Dayton, Ohio: 1971.

Murrow, Casey, and Murrow, Liza. *The Children Come First: Inspired Work of English Primary Schools.* New York: Harper & Row Publishers, 1971.

Olson, Doris. "The Multiage-Multigraded Organization." Mimeographed. Marshall, Minn.: Southwest Minnesota State College.

Evaluation

For Objectives 1 and 2, the learner will complete tasks in writing and submit them to an evaluator.

Quest

Read *Schools Without Failure* by William Glasser (Harper & Row, 1969).

Compac E 4.0405 **Differentiated Staffing**

Context *Organization and Management of the*

Learning Environment

Major Subject *School Organization*

Topic *Differentiated Staffing*

Target Population *Pre-Service and In-Service Elementary*

and Secondary

Behavioral Objectives

1. The learner will define and describe differentiated staffing.
   2. The learner will list three advantages and three disadvantages of differentiated staffing.
   3. In an oral evaluation, the learner will be able to compare and contrast the views of the Association of Classroom Teachers, the Minnesota Federation of Teachers, and the Minnesota Education Association on differentiated staffing.

Prerequisite

Complete Compac A 1.0902 or Block I.

Treatment

Before beginning the compac, elementary teachers should view the slide tape presentation *The Cherry Creek Story* (on the compac support shelf). Pay close attention to the advantages and provisions of differentiated staffing as described in the presentation. Secondary teachers should read "If We Can, Anybody Can" on pages 10-16 of *Differentiated Staffing in Schools* (on shelf).

For Objective 1, read pages 1-9 of *Differentiated Staffing in Schools* and "Differentiated Staffing," pages 21-22, in *Individualizing Instruction and Keeping Your Sanity* by William Bechtol.

For Objective 2, read *Classroom Teachers Speak on Differentiated Teaching Assignments* (on shelf).

For Objective 3, read "ACT Viewpoints," "Will Teachers Design Their Kind of Differentiated Staffing," and "MEA-ACT Position on Differentiated Teaching Assignments" (all in brown folder).

Materials

"ACT Viewpoints." *Today's Education,* March 1969, pp. 60-61.
Bechtol, William. *Individualizing Instruction and Keeping Your Sanity.* Chicago: Follett Publishing Co., 1973.
Minnesota Education Association. "MEA-ACT Position on Differentiated Staffing." St. Paul, Minn.: 1968.
National Education Association. *Classroom Teachers Speak on Differentiated Teaching Assignments.* Washington, D.C., 1969.
Stocker, Joseph. *Differentiated Staffing in Schools.* Washington, D.C.: National School Press, 1970.
Winkels, Henry B. "Will Teachers Design Their Kind of Differentiated Staffing." *Minnesota Teacher,* Spring, 1970.

The Cherry Creek Story. A slide tape. Cherry Creek, Colo.: Cherry Creek Schools, 1970.

Evaluation

For Objectives 1 and 2, the learner will complete the tasks in writing and submit them to an evaluator.

For Objective 3, the learner will compare and contrast, in an oral evaluation, the views of the Association of Classroom Teachers, the Minnesota Federation of Teachers, and the Minnesota Education Association on differentiated staffing.

Compac E 4.0406   **Continuous Progress Education**

Context   *Organization and Management of the*

         Learning Environment

Major Subject   *School Organization*

Topic   *Continuous Progress Education*

Target Population   *Pre-Service and In-Service Elementary*

         and Secondary

Behavioral Objective

After completing the study guide attached to this compac, the learner will be able to discuss with an evaluator a continuous progress, or nongraded, education program, according to the six guidelines stated in the "Evaluation" section of this compac.

Treatment

Complete the study guide attached to this compac (*see* pages 165-66).

Materials

Brown, B. Frank. *The Appropriate Placement School: A Sophisticated Nongraded Curriculum.* West Nyack, N.Y.: Parker Publishing Co., 1965.

Hillson, Maurie, and Bongo, Joseph. *Continuous Progress Education: A Practical Approach.* Palo Alto, Calif.: Science Research Associates, 1971.

Read, Edwin A. "Educational Practice and the Theory of Continuous Pupil Progress." *Audiovisual Instruction,* February 1970.

Thier, Herbert D. "Who's Ready to Try a Birthday School." *Nations Schools,* September 1967.

Ward, Dayton N. "Continuous Progress." *The Texas Outlook,* October 1968.

Wendt, Marilynn, and Boston, Robert E. "Continuous Progress from K to 12." *Michigan Education Journal,* January 1969.

Continuous Pupil Progress. Film. Institute for Development of Educational Activities.

Mathematics Curriculum Guide (1-26) developed by the professional staff of the Tipp City Schools, Tipp City, Ohio.

Evaluation

The evaluation of this compac will be a discussion of continuous progress, or nongraded, education and how it works in an actual school setting. Be prepared to answer the following questions during the course of your discussion with an evaluator (any instructor in the Division of Education).

1. What is continuous progress education and what are some of the reasons for changing from the traditional method to the continuous progress method?

2. What is meant by a continuous progress curriculum guide and what is actually contained in one?

3. What is the process of sequencing in a continuous progress program?

4. Why should a student be diagnosed before he is placed in a continuous progress program?

5. What is the importance of the report card as used in a traditional school in comparison to its use in a continuous progress school?

6. What are the implications or consequences of a continuous progress program on the student?

Study Guide

This study guide is to be used for the purpose of explaining continuous progress, or nongraded, education and how it works in an actual school setting. The materials listed will give the learner a detailed picture of continuous progress education.

Overview

The concept of continuous progress is not new to the education world. This study guide is concerned with a practical approach to introducing continuous progress education to the learner. Some of the things that the learner should accomplish are:

1. gain an overall viewpoint of a continuous progress education program

2. see a continuous progress curriculum program and how it operates

3. describe the process of sequencing

4. explain why the student should be diagnosed for placement purposes

5. explain the concept of recording and reporting in relation to the continuous progress school

6. explain the implications or consequences of a continuous progress program on the student

Treatment

To gain an overall idea of continuous progress, or nongraded, education (statement 1 above), view the 16 mm film *Continuous Pupil Progress*. If more information is needed, read the article "Educational Practice and the Theory of Continuous Pupil Progress" by Edwin A. Read.

For statement 2, study the Curriculum Guide of the Tipp City Schools, Tipp City, Ohio. This is a mathematics curriculum guide (1-26) developed by the professional staff of the Tipp City Schools. Read the introduction to this guide and go through some of the questions at each of the different levels. For a different viewpoint on the curriculum, read chapters 6 and 7 of *The Appropriate Placement School: A Sophisticated Nongraded Curriculum.*

For statement 3, read chapter 2 in *Continuous Progress Education: A Practical Approach* by Maurie Hillson and Joseph Bongo. This chapter deals with sequencing and with developing learning sequences in various areas of the curriculum.

For statement 4, read chapters 3 and 4 in *Continuous Progress Education: A Practical Approach.* These two chapters deal with diagnosis of the student population as a prerequisite to placement in the continuous progress, or nongraded, sequence and construction of learning developmental inventories for screening and for assignments to learning stages. If more information is needed, read the article "Continuous Progress from K to 12."

For statement 5, read chapter 6 in *Continuous Progress Education: A Practical Approach.* This chapter deals with developing appropriate, relevant record keeping and reporting systems for continuous progress programs.

For statement 6, read chapter 8 in *Continuous Progress Education: A Practical Approach.* This chapter deals with questions and answers for the layman concerning continuous progress, or nongraded, programs. Also, read the article "Who's Ready to Try a Birthday School?" by Herbert D. Thier. If more information is needed, read the article "Continuous Progress" by Dayton N. Ward.

Compac E 4.0407	**British Infant School**
Context	*Organization and Management of the*
	Learning Environment
Major Subject	*School Organization*
Topic	*British Infant School*
Target Population	*Pre-Service and In-Service Elementary*

Behavioral Objectives

1. The learner will discuss the process of streaming and why it has been largely abandoned in the British Infant School.

2. The learner will be able to define family or vertical grouping and explain how it works in the British Infant School.

3. The learner will discuss the concept of the integrated day as it is used in the British Infant School.

4. The learner will explain the two fundamental principles that underlie the change from a formal teacher-class relationship to a teacher-child relationship in the British Infant School.

5. The learner will take a subject (preferably in her content area) and discuss how it is taught in the British Infant School.

Prerequisite

None is required.

Treatment

Before starting the objectives, view the film *Primary Education in Great Britain.*

It is suggested that the learner take notes on each objective to be used during the course of evaluation.

For Objectives 1, 2, 3, and 4, read chapters 1 and 3 in *Teaching in the British Primary School* by Vincent Rogers and "The Integrated Day: British Style" by Herbert G. Tag. For additional information, read the book *Family Grouping in the Primary School* or *Crisis in the Classroom: The Remaking in American Education.* More information can be found in the articles "Schools For Children," "How Children Learn," and "Teaching Children to Think" by Joseph Featherstone.

For Objective 5, read one of the chapters, in your content area or other subject area, in the book *Teaching in the British Primary School.* The chapters and the subjects they cover follow:

chapter 5—teaching reading in the Infant School
chapter 6—teaching reading to older children
chapter 7—teaching children to write creatively
chapter 8—the new mathematics
chapter 9—the new science
chapter 10—social and environmental studies
chapter 11—movement, music, drama, and art
chapter 12—modern language

Materials

Featherstone, Joseph. "How Children Learn." *The New Republic,* 2 September 1967.
———. "Schools For Children." *The New Republic,* 19 August 1971.
———. 'Teaching Children to Think." *The New Republic,* 9 September 1967.
Ridgway, Lorna, and Lawton, Irene. *Family Grouping in the Primary School.* New York: Agathon Press, 1969.
Rogers, Vincent R. *Teaching in the British Primary School.* London: Macmillan Co., 1970.
Silberman, Charles E. *Crisis in the Classroom: The Remaking in America Education.* New York: Random House, 1970.
Tag, Herbert G. "Integrated Day: British Style." *Peabody Journal of Education,* July 1971.

Primary Education in Great Britain. Film. Dayton, Ohio: Institute for Development of Educational Activities, 1972.

Evaluation

The learner will discuss with an evaluator the major philosophy of the British Infant School. The learner should cover the following four points during the course of the discussion.

1. Discuss the process of streaming and why it has been largely abandoned in the British Infant School.

2. Define family or vertical grouping and explain how it works in the British Infant School.

3. Discuss the concept of the integrated day as it is used in the British Infant School.

4. Explain the two fundamental principles that underlie the change from a formal teacher-class relationship to a teacher-child relationship in the British Infant School.

The learner will take a subject (preferably in her content area) and discuss how it is taught in the British Infant School.

Notes

Chapter 1

1. Leona E. Tyler, "Individual Differences," *Encyclopedia of Educational Research* (London: The Macmillan Company, 1969), p. 639.
2. Ibid.
3. William Bechtol, "Upgrading—All the Way," *Ohio Department of Elementary School Principals Quarterly,* vol. 3, no. 4 (December, 1967), pp. 12-13.
4. *Individualizing in Schools: The Challenge and the Options* (Washington, D.C.: National School Public Relations Association, 1971), p. 2.
5. Bechtol, op. cit., p. 13.
6. Tyler, loc. cit.

Chapter 2

1. Madeline Hunter, "Dimensions of Nongrading," *Elementary School Journal,* 65 (October, 1964), 20-21.
2. Leonard B. Wheat, "The Flexible Progress Group System," *Elementary School Journal,* 38 (November, 1938), 175.
3. Florence C. Kelley, "The Primary School in Milwaukee," *Childhood Education,* 24 (January, 1948), 236.
4. *Nongraded Schools: NEA Research Memo* (Washington, D.C.: NEA Research Division, 1965), p. 2.
5. William M. Bechtol, "An Analysis of Educational Leadership in Developing a Nongraded School System: A Case Study" (Ed.D. diss., Miami University, 1970), pp. 23-30.
6. Frank R. Dufay, *Ungrading the Elementary School* (West Nyack, N.Y.: Parker Publishing Company, Inc., 1966), p. 24.
7. Doug DeGroote, "Open Education" (speech presented to Kansas State College Teacher Corps, Emporia, Kansas, June, 1972).
8. Mary Lela Sherburne, "The Integrated Day" (address made to the Association of American Publishers, Inc., Washington, D.C., April 28, 1971), pp. 2-4.
9. Robert J. Fisher, *Learning How To Learn: The English Primary School and American Education* (New York: Harcourt Brace Jovanovich, Inc., 1972), pp. 7-9.
I0. *IGE: Multiunit Elementary School* (Madison, Wis.: Wisconsin Research and Development Center for Cognitive Learning, 1971), p. 5.
11. *The Learning Program* (Dayton, Ohio: Institute for Development of Educational Activities, 1970), pp. 3-4.
12. Herbert J. Klausmier et al., *Individually Guided Education in the Multiunit Elementary School: Guidelines for Implementation* (Madison, Wis.: Wisconsin Research and Development Center for Cognitive Learning, 1969), p. 9.
13. Ibid.

14. Jack Frymier (unpublished speech to Western Ohio Elementary School Principals, Dayton, Ohio, October, 1966).

15. Klausmier et al., op. cit.

16. Herbert J. Klausmier et al., *Individually Guided Education and the Multiunit Elementary School: Guidelines for Implementation* (Madison, Wis.: Wisconsin Research and Development Center for Cognitive Learning, 1971), p. 3.

17. *The Learning Program,* op. cit., pp. 3-4.

18. *Nongraded Schools,* op. cit., p. 1.

19. Robert H. Anderson, *Teaching in a World of Change* (New York: Harcourt, Brace, & World, Inc., 1966), p. 83.

20. *IGE Multiage Grouping* (Dayton, Ohio: Institute for Development of Educational Activities, 1971), pp. 7-8.

21. Klausmier et al., op. cit., 1971, pp. 20-23.

Chapter 3

1. Herbert J. Klausmier et al., *Individually Guided Education in the Multiunit Elementary School: Guidelines for Implementation* (Madison, Wis.: Wisconsin Research and Development Center for Cognitive Learning, 1971), p. 17.

2. *Principal's Handbook* (Dayton, Ohio: Institute for Development of Educational Activities, 1971), pp. 31-34.

3. Klausmier et al., op. cit., pp. 16-18.

4. Norman Graper (speech at Regional Conference for IGE Schools, Circle Pines, Minnesota, 1972).

5. Ibid., pp. 15-16.

6. Gerald DiPego, *Unit Operations and Roles* (Dayton, Ohio: Institute for Development of Educational Activities, 1970), pp. 59-64, 84-85.

7. Graper, op. cit.

8. Ibid., p. 17.

9. Norman Graper, "From Rawhide to Mission Impossible" (taped presentation to Minnesota Department of Education, St. Paul, Minnesota, June, 1970).

10. *Principal's Handbook,* op. cit., pp. 16-17.

11. Ibid., pp. 15-16.

12. Ibid., p. 17.

13. Klausmier et al., op. cit., pp. 24-25.

14. Ibid., p. 25.

15. DiPego, op. cit., p. 43.

16. Klausmier et al., op. cit., p. 26.

17. DiPego, op. cit., p. 46.

18. Ibid.

19. *Principal's Handbook,* op. cit., p. 37.

20. Klausmier et al., op. cit., p. 19.

21. *Principal's Handbook,* op. cit., pp. 31-42.

22. Ibid., pp. 45-67.

23. Klausmier et al., op. cit., p. 20.

24. *Principal's Handbook,* op. cit., p. 69.

Chapter 4

1. Robert F. Mager, *Preparing Instructional Objectives* (Palo Alto, Calif.: Fearon Publishers, 1962), p. 2.
2. Ibid., p. 12.
3. Ibid., p. 10.
4. W. James Popham and Eva L. Baker, *Establishing Instructional Goals* (Englewood Cliffs, N.J.: Prentice-Hall, Inc., 1970), p. 13.
5. Mary Quilling, "IGE/MUS-E Assessment" (speech at the IGE Regional Conference, St. Paul, Minnesota, 1972).
6. Ibid.
7. Ibid.
8. Ibid.
9. Ibid.
10. *IGE Performance Testing and Observation,* a filmstrip (Dayton, Ohio: Institute for Development of Educational Activities, 1970).
11. Quilling, op. cit.
12. Wayne Otto and Eunice Askov, *The Wisconsin Design for Reading Skill Development Rationale and Guidelines* (Madison, Wis.: Wisconsin Research and Development Center for Cognitive Learning, 1970), pp. 71-72.

Chapter 5

1. John M. Bahner, *Learning Styles* (Dayton, Ohio: Institute for Development for Educational Activities, 1971), p. 5.
2. Samuel Messick, "The Criterion Problem in the Evaluation of Instruction: Assessing Possible, Not Just Intended, Outcomes," in *Learning Performance and Individual Differences: Essays and Readings,* ed. Len Sperry (Glenview, Ill.: Scott, Foresman and Company, 1972), pp. 100-101.
3. Norman Graper (speech at Regional Conference for IGE Schools, Circle Pines, Minnesota, 1972).
4. Ibid.
5. Adaia Shumsky, "Individual Differences in Learning Styles," in *Learning Performance and Individual Differences: Essays and Readings,* ed. Len Sperry (Glenview, Ill.: Scott, Foresman and Company, 1972), p. 122.
6. Ibid.
7. Ibid., p. 123.
8. Ibid., p. 124.
9. Len Sperry, ed., *Learning Performance and Individual Differences: Essays and Readings* (Glenview, Ill.: Scott, Foresman and Company, 1972), p. 318.
10. Ibid., p. 317.
11. Bahner, op. cit., pp. 18-22.
12. Ibid., p. 19.
13. Ibid., p. 20.

14. Ibid., p. 21.

15. Ibid., p. 22.

16. Sperry, op. cit., pp. 316-19.

17. Graper, op. cit.

18. Ibid.

19. Robert Rosenthal, "Experimenter Expectations," in *Learning Performance and Individual Differences: Essays and Readings,* ed. Len Sperry (Glenview, III.: Scott, Foresman and Company, 1972), pp. 14-23.

20. Sperry, op. cit., p. 319.

21. Herbert J. Klausmier, Dorothy A. Frayer, and Mary R. Quilling, *Individually Guided Motivation: Guidelines for Implementation* (Madison, Wis.: Wisconsin Research and Development Center for Cognitive Learning, 1972), pp. 80-81.

Chapter 6

1. Charles Jung et al., *Interpersonal Communications* (Portland, Oreg.: Northwest Regional Educational Laboratory, 1971), pp. 195-96.

2. Ibid., p. 196.

3. Jack Spatafora and Joan Beugen, *The Learning Program* (Dayton, Ohio: Institute for Development of Educational Activities, 1970), p. 34.

4. Allan A. Glatthorn, "The Small Group," mimeographed, p. 1.

5. Allan A. Glatthorn, *Learning in the Small Group* (Dayton, Ohio: Institute for Development of Educational Activities, 1966).

6. J. Richard Suchman, *Developing Inquiry* (Chicago: Science Research Associates, 1966).

Chapter 7

1. W. James Popham and Eva L. Baker, *Establishing Instructional Goals* (Englewood Cliffs, N.J.: Prentice-Hall, Inc., 1970).

2, *Individualization in Schools: The Challenge and the Options* (Washington, D.C.: National School Public Relations Association, 1971).

3. Don H. Parker, *Schooling for Individual Excellence* (New York: Thomas Nelson and Sons, 1963), pp. 154-57.

4. Ibid., p. 157.

5. Ibid., pp. 159-61.

6. Ibid., p. 156.

7. "What Is a UNIPAC," mimeographed (Anaheim, Calif.: Institute for Development of Educational Activities, 1969), p. 1.

8. William B. Feild and Gardner Swenson, "The UNIPAC: A Form and Process for Individualizing," *Educational Technology,* vol. 12, no. 9 (September, 1972), p. 12.

9. James E. Smith, Jr., "The Learning Activity Package (LAP)," *Educational Technology,* vol. 12, no. 9 (September, 1972), p. 15.

10. Ibid., pp. 15-16.

11. Ibid., p. 15.

12. Martha King, "The Library as a Vital Force in Children's Learning," *Theory Into Practice,* vol. 6, no. 1 (February, 1967), p. 3.

Chapter 9

1. *Communication with Parents,* a filmstrip (Dayton, Ohio: Institute for Development of Educational Activities, 1971).

2. Fred T. Wilhelms, "Evaluation as Feedback," *Evaluation as Feedback and Guide* (Washington, D.C.: Association for Supervision and Curriculum Development, 1967), pp. 10-15.

3. Dr. Bettina King (speech presented to the Nongraded Institute, Miami University, Oxford, Ohio, 1961).

4. John I. Goodlad and Robert H. Anderson, *The Nongraded Elementary School* (New York: Harcourt, Brace & World, 1963), p. 110.

5. *Communication with Parents,* op. cit.

6. Ibid.

Chapter 10

1. James McHolland and Janice Pestrue, "Human Potential Seminars," mimeographed (Evanston, Ill.: Kendall College, 1968).

2. Ibid.

Chapter 11

1. *IGE League Handbook* (Dayton, Ohio: Institute for Development of Educational Activities, 1971), p. 10.

Bibliography

Individualized Instruction

Printed Materials

Anderson, Robert H. *Teaching in a World of Change.* New York: Harcourt, Brace & World, 1966.

Association for Supervision and Curriculum Development Yearbook Committee. *Individualizing Instruction.* Edited by Ronald C. Doll. Washington, D.C.: Association for Supervision and Curriculum Development, 1964.

Bishop, Lloyd K. *Individualizing Educational Systems.* New York: Harper & Row Publishers, 1971.

Drumheller, Sidney J. *Handbook of Curriculum Design for Individualized Instruction: A Systems Approach.* Englewood Cliffs, N.J.: Educational Technology Publications, 1971.

Esbensen, Thorwald. *Working with Individualized Instruction.* Palo Alto, Calif.: Fearon Publishers, 1970.

Hackett, M. G. *Success in the Classroom: An Approach to Instruction.* New York: Holt, Rinehart & Winston, 1971.

Hillson, Maurie, and Bongo, Joseph. *Continuous Progress Education: A Practical Approach.* Palo Alto, Calif.: Science Research Associates, 1971.

Howes, Virgil M. *Individualization of Instruction: A Teaching Strategy.* New York: Macmillan Co., 1970.

———. *Individualizing Instruction in Reading and Social Studies: Selected Readings on Programs and Practices.* New York: Macmillan Co., 1970.

———. *Individualizing Instruction in Science and Mathematics: Selected Readings on Programs, Practices, and Uses of Technology.* New York: Macmillan Co., 1970.

Johnson, Stuart P., and Johnson, Rita B. *Developing Individualized Instructional Materials.* Palo Alto, Calif.: Westinghouse Learning Press, 1970.

Kapfer, Phillip G., and Ovard, Glen F. *Preparing and Using Individualized Learning Packages for Ungraded, Continuous Progress Education.* Englewood Cliffs, N.J.: Educational Technology Publications, 1972.

"Learning Packages," entire issue of *Educational Technology* 12: no. 9 (1972).

Lewis, James, Jr. *Administering the Individualized Instruction Program.* West Nyack, N.Y.: Parker Publishing, 1971.

McNamara, Helen; Carol, Margaret; and Powell, Marvin. *Individual Progression.* Indianapolis: Bobbs-Merrill Co., 1969.

Mager, Robert F. *Preparing Instructional Objectives.* Palo Alto, Calif.: Fearon Publishers, 1962.

National School Public Relations Association. *Individualization in Schools: The Challenge and the Options.* Washington, D.C.: 1971.

Noar, Gertrude. *Individualized Instruction: Every Child a Winner.* New York: John Wiley & Sons, 1972.

Plowman, James W. *Instructional Objectives Exchange.* A project of the Center for the Study of Evaluation. UCLA Graduate School of Education. Los Angeles.

Popham, James, and Baker, Eva. *Establishing Instructional Goals.* Englewood Cliffs, N.J.: Prentice-Hall, 1970.

———. *Planning an Instructional Sequence.* Englewood Cliffs, N.J.: Prentice-Hall, 1970.

———. *Systematic Instruction.* Englewood Cliffs, N.J.: Prentice-Hall, 1970.

Rapport, Virginia, ed. *Learning Centers: Children on Their Own.* Washington, D.C.: Association for Childhood Education International.

Sanders, Norris. *Classroom Questions: What Kinds.* New York: Harper & Row Publishers, 1966.

Sperry, Len, ed. *Learning Performance and Individual Differences: Essays and Readings.* Glenview, Ill.: Scott, Foresman & Co., 1972.

Stahl, D., and Anzalone, P. *Individualized Teaching in the Elementary Schools.* Englewood Cliffs, N.J.: Prentice-Hall, 1970.

Talbert, Gene, and Frase, Larry. *Individualized Instruction: A Book of Readings.* Columbus, Ohio: Charles E. Merrill Publishing Co., 1971.

Voight, Ralph C., et al. *Invitation to Learning: The Learning Center Handbook.* Washington, D.C.: Acropolis Books, 1971.

Weisgerber, Robert. *Developmental Efforts in Individualized Learning.* Itasca, Ill.: F. T. Peacock Publishers, 1971.

Wilhelms, Fred T., ed. *Evaluation as Feedback and Guide.* Washington, D.C.: Association for Supervision and Curriculum Development, 1967.

Films

Continuous Pupil Progress. Dayton, Ohio: Institute for Development of Educational Activities, 1970. (16 mm)

Individualized Learning. Sunnyvale, Calif.: Educational Coordinates, 1971. (16 mm, 12 min.)

Models for Small Group Instruction. Sunnyvale, Calif.: Educational Coordinates, 1971. (16 mm, 12 min.)

More Different Than Alike. Washington, D.C.: National Education Association, 1970. (16 mm, 35 min.)

New Options for Learning. Dayton, Ohio: Institute for Development of Educational Activities, 1971. (16 mm, 22 min.)

Filmstrip and Tape Sets

Appropriate Practice. Los Angeles: VIMCET Associates.

Educational Objectives. Los Angeles: VIMCET Associates.

Establishing Performance Standards. Los Angeles: VIMCET Associates.

Evaluation. Los Angeles: VIMCET Associates.

Individualized Instruction. Washington, D.C.: Department of Audio Visual Instruction. (Set of six filmstrips and tapes.)

Individualized Reading. Los Angeles: Listener Corporation. (Set of five tapes.)

Perceived Purpose. Los Angeles: VIMCET Associates.

Selecting Appropriate Educational Objectives. Los Angeles: VIMCET Associates.

Systematic Decision Making. Los Angeles: VIMCET Associates.

Nongraded Schools

Printed Materials

Beggs, David W., and Buffie, Edward G., eds. *Nongraded Schools in Action.* Bloomington: Indiana University Press, 1967.

Brown, B. Frank. *The Appropriate Placement School: A Sophisticated Nongraded Curriculum.* West Nyack, N.Y.: Parker Publishing, 1965.

Dufay, Frank R. *Ungrading the Elementary School.* West Nyack, N.Y.: Parker Publishing, 1966.

Glogau, Lillian, and Fessel, Murray. *The Nongraded Primary School: A Case Study.* West Nyack, N.Y.: Parker Publishing, 1967.

Goodlad, John I., and Anderson, Robert H. *Nongraded Elementary School.* rev. ed. New York: Harcourt, Brace & World, 1963.

Howard, Eugene R., and Bardwell, R. W. *How to Organize a Non-Graded School.* Englewood Cliffs, N.J.: Prentice-Hall, 1966.

Institute for Development of Educational Activities. *Models for Nongraded Schools: A Report of a National Seminar.* Dayton, Ohio: 1970.

McLoughlin, William P. *Evaluation of the Nongraded Primary.* Jamaica, N.Y.: St. Johns University Press, 1969.

Miller, Richard I. *Nongraded School.* New York: Harper & Row Publishers, 1967.

Rollins, Sidney P. *Developing Non-Graded Schools.* Itasca, Ill.: F. T. Peacock Publishers, 1968.

Smith, Lee L. *A Practical Approach to the Nongraded Elementary School.* West Nyack, N.Y.: Parker Publishing, 1968.

Swidler, Nancy. *Nongrading and the Social Studies One-year School-wide Project Grades K-12.* Chicago: Science Research Associates, 1968.

Tewksbury, John L. *Nongrading in the Elementary School.* Columbus, Ohio: Charles E. Merrill Publishing Co., 1967.

The Nongraded School, a reprint of articles from the November 1967 and January 1968 issues of the *National Elementary Principal.* Washington, D.C.: National Education Association, 1968.

Films

Charlie and the Golden Hamster—The Nongraded Elementary School. Dayton, Ohio: Institute for Development of Educational Activities, 1970. (16 mm, 13 min.)

The Improbable Form of Master Sturm—The Nongraded High School. Dayton, Ohio: Institute for Development of Educational Activities, 1970. (16 mm, 13 min.)

The Open Plan Concept and the Non-graded School. Sunnyvale, Calif.: Educational Coordinates, 1971. (16 mm, 19 min.)

Filmstrip

Nongraded Education: An Overview. Jamaica, N.Y.: Eye Gate House. (four sound filmstrips)

Team Teaching

Printed Materials

Bair, Medill, and Woodward, Richard G. *Team Teaching in Action.* Boston: Houghton Mifflin Co., 1964.

Beggs, David W., ed. *Team Teaching: Bold New Venture.* Indianapolis: Indiana University Press, 1964.

Chamberlin, Leslie. *Team Teaching: Organization and Administration.* Columbus, Ohio: Charles E. Merrill Publishing Co., 1969.

"Cooperative Teaching," entire issue of *National Elementary Principal,* January 1965.

Davis, H. *How to Organize an Effective Team Teaching Program.* Englewood Cliffs, N.J.: Prentice-Hall, 1966.

Hanslovsky, Glenda; Mayer, Sue; and Wagner, Helen. *Why Team Teaching.* Columbus, Ohio: Charles E. Merrill Publishing Co., 1969.

Lobb, M. Delbert. *Practical Aspects of Team Teaching.* Palo Alto, Calif.: Fearon Publishers, 1964.

Moeller, Gerald H., and Mahan, David J. *The Faculty Team.* Chicago: Science Research Associates, 1971.

Polos, Nicholas C. *The Dynamics of Team Teaching.* Dubuque, Iowa: William C. Brown Co., 1965.

York, Jean L. *Philosophy and Background of Team Teaching.* Team Teaching Modules, vol. I. Dallas: Leslie Press, 1971.

———. *The Roles of the Professional and Paraprofessional in Team Teaching.* Team Teaching Modules, vol. 2. Dallas: Leslie Press, 1971.

———. *Materials and Resources Needed for Team Teaching and Individualized Instruction.* Team Teaching Modules, vol. 3. Dallas: Leslie Press, 1971.

———. *Grouping Children for Instruction in Team Teaching.* Team Teaching Modules, vol. 4. Dallas: Leslie Press, 1971.

———. *Team Teaching as a Facilitator of the Nongraded School.* Team Teaching Modules, vol. 5. Dallas: Leslie Press, 1971.

———. *Evaluation of Team Teaching and Children's Continuous Progress.* Team Teaching Modules, vol. 6. Dallas: Leslie Press, 1971.

———. *Prerequisites for Good Planning Sessions in Team Teaching.* Team Teaching Modules, vol. 7. Dallas: Leslie Press, 1971.

Films

Case History of a Teaching Team. Dayton, Ohio: Institute for Development of Educational Activities, 1970. (16 mm, 17 min.)

Team Teaching on the Elementary Level. Hollywood, Calif.: Bailey Films, 1964. (16 mm, 14 min.)

The Quiet Revolution. Washington, D.C.: National Education Association, 1970. (16 mm, 28 min.)

Open Education

Printed Materials

Barth, Roland S. *Open Education and the American School.* New York: Agathon Press, 1972.

Blackie, John. *Inside the Primary School.* London: Her Majesty's Stationery Office, 1967.

Bremer, Anne, and Bremer, John. *Open Education: A Beginning.* New York: Holt, Rinehart & Winston, 1972.

Clegg, Sir Alec. *Revolution in the British Primary Schools.* Washington, D.C.: National Association of Elementary School Principals, 1971.

Cook, Ann. *Open School.* New York: Praeger Publishers, 1973.

Featherstone, Joseph. *Schools Where Children Learn.* New York: Liveright, 1971.

Fisher, Robert J. *Learning How to Learn: The British Primary School and American Education.* New York: Harcourt Brace Jovanovich, 1972.

Frazier, Alexander. *Open Schools for Children.* Washington, D.C.: Association for Supervision and Curriculum Development, 1972.

Grugeon, David, and Grugeon, Elizabeth. *An Infant School.* New York: Citation Press, 1971.

Hasset, Joseph D., and Weisberg, Arline. *Open Education: Alternatives Within Our Tradition.* Englewood Cliffs, N.J.: Prentice-Hall, 1972.

Kohl, Herbert R. *Open Classroom.* New York: Random House, 1970.

Marsh, Leonard. *Alongside the Child: Experiences in the English Primary School.* New York: Harper & Row Publishers, 1972.

Murrow, Casey, and Murrow, Liza. *The Children Come First: Inspired Work of English Primary Schools.* New York: Harper & Row Publishers, 1971.

Nyquist, Edwald, and Haus, Gene, eds. *Open Education: A Sourcebook for Parents and Teachers.* New York: Bantam Books, 1972.

"Perspectives on Open Education," entire issue of the *National Elementary Principal* 12: no. 3 (1972).

Plowden, Lady Bridget, et al. *Children and Their Primary Schools: A Report of the Central Advisory Council for Education.* London: Her Majesty's Stationery Office, 1966.

Rathbone, Charles H., ed. *Open Education: The Informal Classroom.* New York: Citation Press, 1971.

Rogers, Vincent R. *Teaching in the British Primary School.* New York: Macmillan Co., 1970.

Silberman, Charles E. *Crisis in the Classroom: The Remaking in American Education.* New York: Random House, 1970.

Taylor, Joy. *Organizing the Open Classroom: A Teacher's Guide to the Integrated Day.* New York: Schocken Books, 1972.

Weber, Lillian. *English Infant School and Informal Education.* Englewood Cliffs, N.J.: Prentice-Hall, 1971.

Wurman, Richard S., ed. *Yellow Pages of Learning Resources.* Cambridge, Mass.: M. I. T. Press, 1972.

Films

Primary Education in Great Britain. Dayton, Ohio: Institute for Development of Educational Activities, 1972.

The British Infant School—Southern Style. Auburn, Ala.: Promethean Films, 1972.

Filmstrip/Cassette Set

The Open Classroom: Organization and Arrangement. Dayton, Ohio: Institute for Development of Educational Activities, 1972.

Individually Guided Education

The following materials are available from the Institute for Development of Educational Activities, P.O. Box 628, Dayton, Ohio 45419.

Printed Materials

Color Me IGE
IGE Assessment Handbook
IGE Implementation Guide
IGE League Handbook
IGE Learning Program
IGE Overview Brochure
IGE Principal's Handbook
IGE Unit Operations and Roles
Learning Styles
Multiage Grouping

Films

Many Roads
One At A Time, Together
The Unit Meeting
Tuesday—A Day In The Life of An IGE Unit

Filmstrip/Cassette Sets

A Reach for Tomorrow
Building the Learning Program
Home-School Communications
IGE Implementation
IGE Learning Modes
League Linkages
Managing the IGE Learning Environment (I-IV)
Organized for Learning
Performance Testing and Observation
The IGE Learning Program
The IGE Planning System

The following materials are available from the Wisconsin Research and Development Center, 1404 Regent Street, Madison, Wisconsin 53706.

Printed Materials

Elementary School: Guidelines for Implementation
Individually Guided Education and the Multiunit
Individually Guided Motivation: Guidelines for Implementation

Films

Encouraging Independent Reading
Guiding Children as Tutors
Guiding Children Toward Self-Directed Behavior
Individually Guided Education for All Children
Individually Guided Motivation: An Overview
Setting Individual Goals for Learning

Filmstrip/Cassette Sets

Assessment in IGE
Grouping Patterns
IGE/MUS-E Organization and Operation
IGE/MUS-E Roles and Responsibilities
Instructional Programming in IGE

Index